TESTIMONY OF LIGHT

The late FRANCES BANKS, M.A.
(formerly Sister Frances Mary of the Community of
the Resurrection, Grahamstown, South Africa)

TESTIMONY OF LIGHT

by

HELEN GREAVES

Neville Spearman Publishers
The C.W. Daniel Company Limited
1 Church Path, Saffron Walden,
Essex, England

First published in 1969 and subsequently reprinted annually by the Churches' Fellowship for Psychical & Spiritual Studies.

Reprinted in 1977, 1980, 1985, 1986, 1988 (twice), 1990, 1991 (twice), 1993 and 1995 by Neville Spearman Publishers, The C. W. Daniel Company Limited, of Saffron Walden, England.

ISBN 0 85435 164 7

Printed in Great Britain by
Hillman Printers (Frome) Ltd.

Contents

Foreword   *page* 7
Preface   9
Biographical Introduction   13

Part I
The Return   21
The Scripts   27

Part II
Explanation   129
Second Series of Scripts   132

An Interview with the late Sir Malcolm Sargent on B.B.C.
April 19th 1968

Transcribed from a recording by Radio Direction Telediphone Unit

SIR MALCOLM SARGENT: "I feel death, which I've never been afraid of, which I look forward to . . ."
INTERVIEWER: "You look forward to death?"
SIR MALCOLM SARGENT: "Oh, very much. Er . . . Obviously. I mean this life has been wonderful and because I've loved this life so much, I know I shall love death more. Don't you remember, He said, 'When I came to this world, I do not remember a moment but I was not a stranger'. . . . So shall it be when one passes from life to death, from life to life . . ."

(By kind permission of Sir Malcolm's Secretary.)

Foreword

Lieut.-Col. R. M. Lester

(*Author of "In Search of the Hereafter", etc., Founder and Vice-President of The Churches' Fellowship for Psychical & Spiritual Studies*)

Telepathy between the living is now generally accepted, but telepathy between the living and the so-called 'dead' is less common. Countless books have been written recording alleged communication with discarnate minds and many of these are very dubious in their authenticity.

Such communications are claimed to have been received by a variety of methods—automatic writing; clairaudience; trance mediumship and so on.

The highest level of communication is undoubtedly that of telepathy and in this book we have an outstanding example of this, where communion between two people on either side of the veil has been achieved without effort—and without seeking —in a very beautiful manner.

I have known Helen Greaves for many years, not only as an experienced writer, but also as one versed in the higher studies of mysticism and possessing a gift that enables her to penetrate to the next dimension of consciousness.

The communicator, Frances Banks, was also well known to me, and she shared very actively in our work of the Churches' Fellowship for Psychical & Spiritual Studies. She was held in the highest esteem by all who had the privilege of meeting her and it is no surprise to us that one of her early tasks after passing from this life was to contact the mind of one with whom she had worked so closely while in the physical body.

By using Helen Greaves as a pure, unobstructed 'channel' Frances Banks has been able to get such a wonderful "Testimony of Light" across that—as the 'author' states—it "will bring com-

7

fort to many and stimulate faith and hope in many" who, in this materialistic age, are feeling frustrated and despairing.

Those of us who know both Helen Greaves and Frances Banks so well, are impressed by the authenticity of these scripts. The phrasing and content of the communications are so typical of Frances, and completely unlike the style of writing as shown by the 'author' in her previous books and articles.

Transition to the next stage of consciousness has not changed Frances Banks in any way, except—as she says—to have progressed to "a little more illumination".

Her message—that the death of the body is but a gentle passing to a much freer and fuller life, comes across with great clarity and conviction.

Preface

CANON J. D. PEARCE-HIGGINS, M.A., HON.C.F.

(A Vice-Chairman of The Churches' Fellowship for Psychical and Spiritual Studies)

It is a privilege of which I am quite unworthy, to be asked to write a foreword to this remarkable book containing communications claimed to come from Frances Banks through the intermediacy of her friend Helen Greaves, and which, from my own personal acquaintance of Frances certainly, to me bear all the stamp of authenticity. If they are indeed from her, then she truly has 'outsoared the shadow of our night' as one would have expected.

I have used the word 'intermediacy' rather than 'mediumship' because this book would appear to contain the ideal form of communication, namely between two minds, which already on earth were well in tune with each other, and appear, though parted physically to have been able to continue in 'unity of the spirit' across the gap of death.

I have been asked to comment on the fact that Frances occasionally refers to Reincarnation, since such references may be a stumbling-block to Christian readers, few of whom, unless they are scholars, probably are aware that there was a 500-year tradition of such belief within the early Church itself; mainly in the Alexandrian school, including such names as Clement, Justin Martyr, St. Gregory of Nyssa, and most notable of all, Origen, who had a well worked out reincarnational system of belief, which certainly makes sense, and avoids many of the objectionable features of oriental versions. Further, it is far from clear that the Church ever officially rejected such belief, however little the medieval mind was able to contain it. The Council of Constantinople in A.D. 553, at which it seems that a corrupt form of Origen's teaching was anathematised, is held by many

9

historians to have been imperfectly constituted—the Pope him-self refused to be present—and even Roman Catholics contest its validity as a General Council.

The Church today has got to face the fact that in our shrunken world, with the eastern cultures on our doorstep, Reincarnation is again a life issue, since according to Geoffrey Gorer's sociologi-cal study ('In search of English character' 1955) some 12 per cent of our population believe in it, as against 10 per cent who accept traditional Christian and biblical eschatology, and the spread of the belief continues. Rudolf Steiner, one of the most powerful scientific intellects and spiritual geniuses of our race, in his entirely Christo-centric 'Anthroposophy', has Reincarna-tion as central also to his teaching. The records of that humble Christian seer and healer, the late Edgar Cayce in U.S.A. contain many references to Reincarnation (in connection with sickness in this life—and recently Dr. Guirdham has been pur-suing the same idea in dealing with mental illness). From the empirical angle Dr. Ian Stevenson and other investigators con-tinue to collect evidence some of which appears extremely sug-gestive of the possibility that individual cases do occur, even though Reincarnation may not necessarily be a general rule for all. Since so many of our eschatological beliefs appear to rest largely on wishful thinking (else how could there be so many different and conflicting views on the market?) the touchstone of experience and experiment is important if we are to avoid talking nonsense, and this book would therefore seem to contain relevant material to this study. We note also that Reincarna-tion was in the air in New Testament times—how could it have been otherwise in the Greco-Roman culture, heir of the Py-thagorean-Platonic tradition, of three thousand years of Egyptian religion, and increasingly making contacts with the East? Some of the words attributed to Jesus, notably in connec-tion with John Baptist give evidence of the currency of the idea.

Should we accept these communications as authentic we then run into the vexed problem of 'Revelation'—but then Frances was always a controversial figure! The Church rightly has held that there can be no NEW revelation, and that nothing can supersede the supreme revelation of divine love in the person of Jesus Christ, but it has never been very happy with the idea that there might be supplementary revelation, shedding light upon the details and working out of the divine love. Further we have the regrettable fact that Frances was a woman! Yet we learn of the respect paid to the prophetess Huldah in the reign of Josiah, and of the importance she played in the (then) new revelation in 721 B.C. which we know as the book 'Deuteronomy'; we love and respect Mother Julian for her 'Revelations of divine love'—we can learn from an Evelyn Underhill or a Simone Weil, and I feel sure that *Testimony of Light* must rank with these—certainly as being worthy of the most careful study as being a manifestation of the working of the Spirit in our own time and day, 1969.

It is this task of study which the Churches' Fellowship exists to promote, and therefore has no hesitation in sponsoring this book for individual study and assessment of its value.

Biographical Introduction

The 'scripts' in this book have, I believe, been communicated to me by telepathy and inspiration from the surviving mind of Frances Banks, M.A., who left this world on November 2nd, 1965.

No doubt this will be challenged as a bold statement. I make it in perfect faith and with integrity.

If the reader has studied my book *The Dissolving Veil*, published in 1967 by the Churches' Fellowship for Psychical & Spiritual Studies, he will realise that this work of telepathy and communication 'between the worlds' was not a work of my choosing. The Extra Sensory Perceptions of clairaudience and telepathy which have been developed into a receiving-set for these communications were never sought by me. I do not use these perceptions professionally, or for personal gain of any sort.

Frances Banks was an intimate friend of mine. For the last eight years of her life we worked together psychically and spiritually. We also explored the deep levels of meditation.

Miss Banks was an outstanding woman in many fields of endeavour. For twenty-five years she was a Sister in the Anglican Community of the Resurrection in South Africa, and during much of that time, she was Principal of the Teachers' Training College in Grahamstown. She was the author of many books on psychology; one on the education of prisoners, *Teach Them to Live* (after some years of experience as Tutor-organiser at Maidstone Gaol); and her last book was *Frontiers of Revelation*, being an account of researches into psychic and mystical phenomena.

Those who knew Frances Banks intimately will recognise her 'signature' in these scripts. In her earthly life she was a pioneer and she exhibits, by her frank communication and interpretation of her life in the spiritual realms, that she still merits that

13

epithet. She was ever striving to learn, to discover and then to impart that which she had made her own to others when she lived among us; and she has carried this characteristic with her into the Beyond.

Frances had indicated that these 'accounts' which are of an inspirational teaching nature should be made public, in the hope that a firsthand report of that next phase of living to which we are all graduating, may be of value.

For a description of Frances' early life and her graduation into the teaching profession, we can refer to her own account in *Frontiers of Revelation*; we can read between the lines in assessing her early dedication to the life of the spirit. Her 'conversion' as she told it to me, to High Anglican adherence, came through the influence on her thought of a well-known cleric, Father Trevelyan at Bournemouth when she was in her early twenties. The day of her decision to devote her life to God and missionary work in His Church was a red-letter day in her spiritual progress. Hers was a deep and penetrating intellect, and here was a challenge. In the words of that great Seeker after Truth, Francis Bacon, she vowed, 'I will find where Truth is hid, though it were hid indeed within the Centre'. This dedication was to be the future motive of her whole existence, taking her into the religious life, and then, after twenty-five years of Community work, bringing her out again into the world to study, to investigate, and indeed 'to leave her stamp on everything she touched', as one of her admirers expressed it.

In the Community of the Resurrection at Grahamstown in South Africa, which she joined, she was immediately assigned to teaching in the Training College for Teachers under the Cape Provincial Education Department, and, excepting for six months at an African training college in the Transvaal, and visits to England for refresher courses, she spent the rest of her twenty-five years in religion, teaching at this college. In the course of her teaching-life, she taught teaching method, psychology, English and art.

Realising that her B.A. degree would not be sufficient for advanced teaching and the filling of more responsible posts, Frances asked for, and obtained, permission to study psychology at Rhodes University, which was almost next door to the convent. She obtained an M.A. degree in the subject, specialising in child psychology and educational psychology. Later, she wrote and published text books on these subjects which, I understand, are still in use in training colleges in Africa.

I recall that Frances was amusingly perceptive to me about these days of university studentship amidst convent life.

"It was difficult to adapt myself", she said, "from the modern ideas and techniques of university lectures to the almost medieval community life. These were two worlds entirely; sometimes I had to smile to myself at the advanced modernity of my studies in contrast to the ancient undeviating rule of the religious life."

But she did adapt. Whatever her private conflicts she persisted. She obtained her degree and she stayed a convent Sister and a teacher at the training college. Such a triumph must have cost her dear, but it illustrates a further light on the strength of that deep inner life in Frances, which made her a seeker all her days. Indeed, from these scripts we see that she is still seeking Truth and Reality that are the foundation of all existence.

Seeking and Service coloured all her life from the young schoolteacher, to Sister Mary for fifteen years Principal of the training college in Grahamstown; to Miss Banks, M.A., Tutor-Organiser at Maidstone Prison, Kent, from which experience stemmed her book, *Teach Them to Live* which the late Lord Birkett described as an 'important contribution to our social history'; to the Frances Banks who delved into the levels of Extra Sensory Perception, lectured for the Churches' Fellowship for Psychical & Spiritual Studies, and indeed was responsible for the introduction of the word 'spiritual' into the Fellowship's name; to Frances Banks, author of *Frontiers of Revelation*, which has become a classic of its kind.

Here were seventy-two years of a dedicated life—a questioning mind ever alert to the possibility of uniting psychology with religion, of discovering the mobile centre of consciousness in man, and with a deep inner longing for union with soul and spirit. Such a life must have been many lives in one, many experiences enjoyed or suffered to enrich a fine soul in its earthly pilgrimage.

Yet Frances had the faults of such a personality. She had a will of iron; it carried her through tests and trials, but it also made her obstinate and obdurate about her personal points of view. She was fearless and outspoken in usually perceptive criticisms. That she 'used' her will-power to influence others may be a controversial point with her critics; she certainly challenged people to become something greater, and she could project herself and her thought so strongly that sometimes she aroused antagonism. A woman of her strength of character could not be accepted mildly. Yet her insight levelled her concentration on people with a potential: she rarely bothered with weak characters.

This is illustrated in a statement from a former student, Mary Jordaan, who writes:

"Her [Frances'] look seemed to challenge one, to dare one to be someone. Perhaps that is why, even her admirers would admit that 'Fanny' could be harsh in her criticisms. She didn't suffer fools gladly, yet it wasn't so often the weak student who suffered at Fanny's hands, as a student with a potential who was prepared to waste her gifts. . . ."

From Alan Paton, author of *Cry the Beloved Country* comes this impression:

"I first met Sister Frances Mary when we were having a course in religious education at the convent there. My impression was that this was a woman of tremendous force of character and tremendous will-power. I would guess that this happened somewhere in the early 1940's. . . . I was soon aware that she had concentrated her tremendous will on me. I think that she regarded me as a person to be won over and I could feel this concentration throughout the whole week that we were there, so much so, in fact, that I became conscious of an eagle-like quality in her. . . ."

A tribute to the great work done by Frances Banks in South Africa is also given by Miss Margaret Snell, a former colleague in religious education, and at one time acting editor for *Christian Education.*

She writes:

"Her [Frances'] work in South Africa was a big one. Of her contribution to educational matters in general I am not qualified to speak, but she was always rushing across to Cape Town to serve on some committee or other of the Cape Education Department.

"Likewise on religious education, which was the ground on

which we first met in 1941—her influence and inspiration were felt as far north as Lusaka, and I doubt, without the tremendous enthusiasm she aroused for a new look and meaning in the presentation of eternal truth, the Christian Education Movement would ever have got off the ground at all. Her deepest influence was on individual lives. In the years of my travels, whenever I met a dedicated and devoted teacher, how often did I find she had done her training under 'Fanny', as her students called her, and again and again I have heard how decisive and permanent her inspiration was. We shall not meet her like again, but from such a soul there is no real parting. . . ."

To Frances I owe a great spiritual debt. We founded a group of men and women for the study and practice of Group Meditation for World Goodwill. This Group still continues, and has been extended into four other such groups with a fifth forming at the time of writing. Members of these groups testify to the real help they have received from this practice and to the extension of consciousness which it has brought to each one; and we are still very aware of Frances' continued interest and participation. Frances was the brains and the organiser in our partnership; I was able, humbly to supply at times the counsel of the 'Inner Voice'. Sometimes together we experienced the sense of Presence of Great Ones, and were refreshed and uplifted thereby. Thus we were not surprised when one day a former beloved Mother Superior of the Order, Mother Florence, 'communicated'; as did also Father Joseph White, a priest from the Society of the Sacred Mission, who had conducted Community Retreats at the convent. Frances recognised him instantly from descriptions, and was much encouraged by his continued interest in her work. Thus, there was no astonishment in the reunion of Frances with these fine souls in her next life. In her last illness, when she lay in a London hospital, I told her that I felt Mother Florence was with her. I recall her calm smile. "I know! Last night I *saw* Mother Florence distinctly beside my bed."

A beautiful little book, entitled *Four Studies in Mysticism* by Frances Banks, M.A., was published posthumously by the Mysticism Committee of the Churches' Fellowship in 1967. These studies of St. Teresa of Avila, St. John of the Cross, Plotinus and Pierre Teilhard de Chardin were written by Frances as a prelude to the book we were to write together on our practical findings in the study of mysticism. That book was never written. In its stead this *Testimony of Light* in which I have co-operated with her, has come into being after her death.

In a foreword to *Four Studies in Mysticism,* the Bishop of Crediton wrote:

"I did not know Frances Banks well. I met her on three occasions, and I 'sat under her' once, but I realised, as soon as I talked with her, that here was a rare soul who had vision, a deep knowledge of the spiritual life, an adventurous spirit which never clouded her serenity and a humility and sense of proportion which made her a ministering servant rather than an infallible and cocksure teacher. I am happy to write this foreword to these Studies in Mysticism. Frances Banks wrote nothing which she herself had not experienced at deep levels and I have no doubt that those who read her last words will rise up and call her blessed."

Could there be a better summing-up of her life and work?

PART I

The Return

Frances Banks died, as she had lived, fully conscious of what she was doing and where she hoped to go. She refused drugs until the very end, bearing her pain with fortitude. At the last she spoke of seeing incarnate and discarnate entities in her room. She arranged her material affairs and said 'farewell' to those of her friends who were near enough to visit her. She astonished the good Scottish doctor who attended her at the last by saying cheerfully, a day or so before she lapsed into a coma:

"Goodbye, Doctor. See you in the next world!"

Her brave words to me, "You know I have cancer. I will not get over this", indicated that she had accepted and was ready for the next phase. She was even eager, for I am told by those who looked after her, that she would wake in the morning and sigh:

"Am I still here? I had hoped to have gone."

At the end her breath was laboured and she lapsed into unconsciousness. Yet for the flash of a second she drew herself back so that she spoke normally and with control. This was in a poignant incident on the day before her death, and it illustrates clearly her consciousness of herself as a soul, as well as a mind and body; and a soul and mind that would live on in another dimension after they had left a sick body. This story, I feel, has a bearing on the next section of this book, in which Frances' mind was able to impress mine, and so further the message which she so eagerly wished to impart, the message of assurance of the continued life and progress of the soul.

Frances had been in and out of coma for nearly two days when I received, by the morning mail, a tiny bottle of water. With it came a letter relating that this phial of water had been brought, by the writer, from Lourdes. It was, she wrote, holy water from the Spring at Lourdes. Could I anoint Frances with it? There *might* be a miracle! In any case, it would be helpful.

I asked permission to carry out this wish and was granted it. I took the bottle, and having been warned that our patient was in a coma, or asleep, I tiptoed in. Frances was propped up by pillows, ill and shrunken. Her eyes were closed. She was very still except for the laboured indrawing of her breath. I stood for a moment at the end of the bed, watching her. Slowly her eyes opened. Recognition dawned. She smiled without speaking. Then the eyelids dropped again.

Leaning over her I whispered:

"This is holy water from Lourdes, Frances."

With it I made the Sign of the Cross on her forehead and the palms and backs of her hands. She only moaned. I stood beside her and prayed silently that she might go peacefully to that new life to which she looked forward so eagerly.

After a minute, without opening her eyes, she murmured in a dreamy voice:

"It's all right, my dear. *The Change has started.*"

Then she lapsed immediately into unconsciousness. The next day, at lunch time, she simply stopped breathing. Her soul had gone on its new pilgrimage.

At the Cremation Service, at which the Reverend Richard Hall officiated, many of the mourners were 'aware' of her presence.

At the Memorial Service in London, which was conducted by The Reverend Canon J. D. Pearce-Higgins, M.A., HON.C.F., Vice-Chairman of The Churches' Fellowship for Psychical & Spiritual Studies, I 'saw' her in her nun's habit in company with her beloved Mother Florence, a past Mother Superior of the Order. This was afterwards verified by others present who had also 'seen' her and who spoke of the habit of the Order in which she appeared to be clothed.

After her death I felt cut off from all spiritual contact. My mind was dry and arid. For some weeks I found it most difficult to meditate, or even to withdraw into the quietness of the soul at all.

Then one evening, a Sunday, about three weeks after Frances' death, as I was sitting alone beside my fire listening to radio music, I gradually became aware of a Presence. The air seemed to take on a great stillness and a hush of expectancy. I switched off the radio and allowed myself to relax into this peace. No thought of a possible communicator from another world occurred to me. No word was spoken in my mind. I was very still and quiescent. Slowly my whole being seemed to be caught up into a peace and beauty that I cannot describe. This beauty was both around me and within me. Almost imperceptibly I passed into a state of deep meditation in which I was conscious of being immersed in light. I was part of the Light yet the Light issued from beyond me. I felt a One-ness with all that was highest and best and with the eternal Self within me. I felt the nearness of spiritual Presences. I was swept on into a meditation in which Frances and I had participated some years before. I even heard my mind repeating invocations from that meditation . . .

Gently, and with great reverence, it was borne in upon me that I was not only in touch with my own immortal soul, but also with the soul of Frances Banks.

This was Communion, silent, still, uplifting; a Communion emptied of all personality challenges, of all limiting human conceptions. This was Communion at soul level. I felt lifted out of myself into wonder and love and light.

The experience lasted for about a half-hour. Then it slowly faded. I sat on, utterly at peace, with no thoughts threading through the stillness of my mind. I did not even try to analyse what had happened in this immortal moment; I was content to 'be'.

It was only after I had, later, gone into the kitchen and was making coffee that an exhilaration such as I had never known flooded my mind. I found myself saying aloud, half in amazement, but wholly in gladness.

"That was the *soul* of Frances—not just her mind. We communed at soul-level . . ."

It was some days later when I felt Frances' *mind* impinging on mine, as it had often done in our time together on earth. Words dropped into my thoughts which did not come from my consciousness. I knew that her discarnate mind and my incarnate one had linked together again in telepathic communication.

Frances had something to say! She wished to get her message across. I was the one who had been her 'Celestial Telephone' as she had called it. What more natural than that she should wish now to speak and not merely to listen? She was now in the position of 'seeing a little farther'.—I knew, from my personal experience of her, that Frances never wasted a minute when she could be about her Father's business. Now that she was evidently restored to consciousness and awareness after the change into her new life, her first burning desire would be to make known all that was happening; to *send back* at first-hand. She would now be able to demonstrate the next life, of which she had written and spoken; to expound with authority on the subject which had been close to her heart; the reality of Life Everlasting; the continued progress of the Spirit . . .

I sat down, took my pen and began to write. Words, thoughts, sentences tumbled out on to the paper. It was almost as though I took dictation. Yet this was *not* automatic writing. I was perfectly in control. I could *feel* that her mind was using mine. This was a composite effort. Her mind 'inspired' the subject matter, the experiences and later, the stories of her fellow-travellers in the Life Beyond. She explored the potentials of my mind, and enabled me to employ the craft of writing which I had learned in my journalistic work. To me it seems to have been the perfect partnership of mind and mind, which we had never actually achieved whilst she was in the earth body. This fact has been made more clear to me by the reactions of the Reverend Bertram E. Woods, Honorary Secretary of The Churches' Fellowship for Psychical & Spiritual Studies, who read the manuscript.

At a further period in the writing of the scripts, Frances explained that she herself was working with, and under the inspiration of, a group, or band, for this transmitting of her impressions of the Life Beyond to be translated into a book.

Later, as I became more used to this method, I was even able to ask a question and receive an immediate answer. I wrote for an hour. My pen scarcely lifted from the page. When I read through what I had written my astonishment grew. This happened for several days and I became more astounded at the subjects upon which I had written. I could not, without effort and without definitely searching my limited imagination, have invented such stories as poured through me.

Time after time my pen wrote. There was hardly a correction made in all the hundreds of words written, though I was never aware of what I was going to write. Yet my life went on normally enough. I still saw my friends, enjoyed watching television, read, shopped, drove about the countryside and was not aware of any *personal* communications from Frances between sessions. It was exactly as though I was simply registering and translating her thoughts at certain times.

Yet when I read aloud some of the scripts to a friend living near I was as astonished as was she that the stories were so fresh and intriguing; as if I had never been employed to write them!

During this time though, I was perfectly aware that I was 'under compulsion' to carry on with the work until all that she wished had been communicated. Frances' persistent dedication was still in evidence—I was the one most able to do what she wanted and what I realised she felt was the crowning of her earthly mission. Therefore she concentrated on me. I must admit I cringed as I envisaged the publicity to come, for I knew that she intended publication. Often I wondered how I would face the criticism and possible ridicule such a book would arouse . . .

But Frances' strong will persisted; it was, as ever, the Will-to-Good. These revelations must go out in the spirit of Service in which they were sent into manifestation. Her dedicated Self swept aside all obstacles I might put in their way.

"Many may ridicule", she insisted, "but if only a few are strengthened in consciousness, and helped to live closer to Reality, then our partnership has not been in vain."

With this I must be content.

That Sunday experience of soul-to-soul communion has not been repeated; indeed it must be a rare occurrence, and I was most blessed even to have known it once. But the communications have gone on to the end and they now lie here on my desk, typed for publication.

But Frances has proved even more than communication. She has shown to be possible that which she always advocated so strongly, *that psychic and spiritual communication are but different levels of one spiral;* that communion is of the spirit, and therefore of a higher level than psychic interpenetration or extra-sensory perception; that both methods will be demonstrable in the New Age now approaching; and that the higher communion is to be opened through meditation and contact with the deep centre of man.

Frances always believed this. She was convinced of the fact of communion with the spiritual worlds and of the reality of the higher self in each one of us. She trusted implicitly in the survival of mind and personality beyond death and she was reverently aware of the spirit within which urged her on—the Christ-in-You of Christianity.

Always she strove for a 'break-through' to Spirit, and by this, I do not mean only psychic communication. Her belief was that, through meditation, through retiring into the deep centre of oneself and finding the place of the silence of the soul, communion could be established with advanced souls; higher beings, great ones whom we call Saints. This is the true communion of Saints; a One-ness with the Divine Company of Heaven, resulting in a new intuitive perception of unity and inspiration for radiant living.

This, she felt, was the message for the New Age into which we are now emerging, a greater extension of man's consciousness, so that even during the limitation of earthly life, he can enter the beauty of the spiritual worlds and receive inspiration therefrom. She stressed, also, that man should realise and accept his place in a divine scheme. She believed intensely with the forward-looking thought of Pierre Teilhard de Chardin that, as he phrased it, "Co-extensive with their Without, there is a Within to things". She also believed that 'the last enemy that shall be destroyed is Death'.

In the testimony which follows, Frances continues her mission. She has shown her experience of death and the change into a new conception of living, illustrating this with poignant stories of the effects of the death-change on others with whom she has been brought into contact. She gives us freely of her further knowledge of the progress of the soul outwards, upwards and forwards into Divinity.

The Scripts

... I have been able to come to you; your husband over here has brought me. Yes. I know him well now. I always felt a kinship with him, even when I was on earth. Do you remember? I like him. He has a great sense of humour—a kind or irrepressible fun. You two must have enjoyed each others' company....

I am in a kind of rest home now. It is run by the Sisters of the community to which I belonged when in incarnation. They are so kind and gentle with me. I am now lying in a bed, high up on a terrace, that looks out over a vast sunlit plain. It is a beautiful scene, and so restful. ... I am recuperating from the illness which brought disintegration to my physical body. I feel content and calm and at peace. I shall stay here. ... Indeed I have already told Mother Florence that I want to work with her here when I am ready....

Souls are brought here from earth and from other places (but I do not know much of those places)—when they are ready. They are 'nursed' and taken care of here, as am I. ... After I have become adjusted to this life I think I shall stay on here and teach with the Sisters, if they will have me! And if I can really be useful. ... You see how my 'earth psychology' will come in useful, together with the explanations of the further stages of progress, when I have learnt more myself. How I shall enjoy co-relating the two 'psychologies' in any classes I have, and in individual talks! It is going to be rather like a return to the prison work I did at Maidstone Gaol, only of course, on a different level. ... Here, there is no compulsory confinement, and no punishment, except what you mete out to yourself! You can come and go of course . . . but I realise already that you can only 'go' elsewhere, when you are ready....

I am so glad that I can continue to work. One loves to be useful, and I always loved my work, as you well know. Here, later on, I feel that I can put much of what I have experienced to good use. It will help me too. . . . I have always been, by nature and inclination, a teacher, and it is a great joy to learn that one can still exercise one's skills in this new life. It will be good for me too, to do a job of work where I am not noticed. . . . Beware of becoming noticed too much. . . . Therein lies temptation. . . .

I have met Father Joseph, our 'Dominic'. He is a wonderful person. He seems to emanate such goodness, love and strength. When I first became aware of him, I was immediately reminded of your description when you first saw him clairvoyantly . . . 'rangy'. Certainly his 'body' is tall and loosely built. He wore the same brown habit with the red girdle, just as he used to wear when I first contacted him as our Retreat Priest in the Community.

I'll try to tell you what happened:

After the Change was over and I was free of my earthly 'covering' I 'woke up' here in this hospital of the Rest Home. My room had no walls and the sunlight seemed to flow over one all the time. I opened my eyes . . . or I came back to consciousness . . . and there was Mother Florence just as she used to be and as I had remembered her for so many years.

She took my hand. She said "So you have arrived safely?"

But I must have been very weary, for I can remember little more. I think I slept again.

A long time later . . . it *seemed* a long time later, I found myself lying here gazing out at this tranquil and beautiful scene around me.

Suddenly I 'knew' that someone was beside me. I looked round and gave my attention to this new idea.

There was Father Joseph just as I had always remembered him. He sat down beside me and took my hand in his.

"Well, Sister?" he said.

That was all. Just "Well, Sister?", as if we were both back in my study in the college in South Africa. I felt such power and strength flow out from him. I think I must have wept . . . it was all too wonderful. . . .

He didn't say much, or I was too tired to pay attention. For

I must have drifted into sleep again. When I gathered my thoughts together again to speak to him—he had gone. . . .

But he'll come again. Mother Florence tells me now that he comes quite often to see her patients. Oh! but I shall not be a patient here for long you know!

As soon as I can re-orient myself sufficiently, I shall be teaching or tutoring again. It is the service I can give . . . I'm already learning so much . . . I have discovered that I can use telepathy *both ways*, to receive and to relay. There are not the difficulties here that we experienced on the earth. This holds out all sorts of exciting possibilities. Indeed I am already able to contact your mind, and what is more important, to *hold* that contact so as to *pour ideas* out to you! This has infinite possibilities. . . .

I'll try to come to your group. I know that you are meeting. Everything it seems is known here. . . . I must break off now . . . I will 'talk' to you again . . . I begin to know you now in quite a different way. . . . I see your 'light'. . . .

Later

You remember that, when I was in the body, I once said to a prisoner at Maidstone (following a discussion on the possibility of life after death): "A minute after you die you will be exactly the same!"

You recall, also, that that very statement was the first psychic message you gave me? You spoke the name of this prisoner who had died soon after my talk, without our meeting again, and you said "He wants me to tell you that the last words you ever said to him were absolutely true. . . ."

Well. I reiterate this statement (now that I too have made the transition), in full agreement with all that was implied in it. *For it is so.* As soon as I was able to bring myself to a conscious state of mind, after my withdrawal from my worn-out body, I knew that I was the *same in essence*. True, I felt light, and there was a new sense of freedom that was bewildering.

I was the same . . . yet not the same!

With a flash of realisation I decided that I must be stone deaf, for I could no longer hear any of the usual sounds of everyday life, the chatter and movement of human beings around me; the whistles of trains, the twittering of birds. . . . There were no noises in this new consciousness. One of my first recollections was "I am still conscious. *The Change has taken place . . .* but I cannot hear, neither can I see!"

And for a space of time I seemed to lose my identity. . . . I recall endeavouring anxiously to pierce through this new state to recall memory.

"Who am I? What did I do?"

It was a strange; almost eerie experience, for the name I had borne for over seventy years eluded me. . . . At length I recall telling myself to "Give it up and go to sleep" and, in a way, this is what I must have done. At least consciousness went from me. I remembered nothing more. How long this went on I have no possible way of knowing . . . perhaps in earth time, for a very short space.

But when next I came back to consciousness I seemed to be pulling myself up out of a thin sea of silver. . . . Those are the only words I can use to describe the experience.

And the first face I saw was the smiling one of my dear Mother in religion—Mother Florence. I was so overwhelmed I couldn't speak. . . . From then on I remember that I seemed to be in and out of consciousness. . . . But now I found that I was lying in an open porch with a vista of blue and silver before me. . . . This was beautiful beyond words and calming to my spirit. Trouble, anxiety and all sense of loss abated; a great feeling of peace enwrapped me.

"*This is it*" I kept assuring myself in wonder, "I have made The Change!" I realised then that I could both see and hear as before, only now in a more *intense* way. I thought immediately, "I wonder whether I can 'get through'. I must tell Helen about this . . ."

Later, as I grew more accustomed to this new consciousness, I was able to 'commune' (I cannot explain this by any of our former terms), with both Mother Florence and Father Joseph. How delighted I was to meet them! And to know that Father Joseph was indeed the same splendid, wise soul I had known, in my Community days. . . . He was again able to help me much. He gave me confidence. . . .

I felt as if I was 'convalescing' . . . as indeed I suppose I was from the effects of my last painful illness. . . .

It was borne in on my thoughts that an 'aura' of sadness surrounded me. "They will be burning my body" I said to myself.

Immediately an intense *desire* filled me to be again with all those friends I had loved and those who had loved me, at this solemn ceremony.

In an inexplicable way, and due no doubt to my intense desire, I was able to be present with you all in mind and consciousness, *whilst still lying here in this silvery light.* I wondered if this was what astral travelling must have been like. . . . But it was a wonderful experience. . . .

I 'saw' you all . . . I was grateful to those who had journeyed to Maidstone to be present at these last rites. I gloried in the beautiful flowers. I wanted to weep at Richard's mystical interpretation of the change which had separated me (though only seemingly) from you all. I longed to say 'thank you' to those who had made my last days on earth comfortable. I 'read' the thoughts of Bertram Woods that the Fellowship was losing a tireless worker. I felt 'lifted up' in mind and soul because I was being missed, because there was so much affection and because Richard was wisely making this a hopeful farewell, without the heavy burden of emphasised sorrow and mourning which would have saddened and distressed me.

Then, just as inexplicably as I had become part of these scenes, it all faded. I was lying here, at peace.

"So this is death!" I recall saying to one of the Sisters who was beside me—"*Life separated by density*—that is all!"

Elation filled me. I knew now that I could 'tune in' and even 'see' the earthplane, if desire was strong enough to loosen the barrier between your world and my new one. The possibility rested with me. . . . This, I realised, was my first lesson. . . . Now I dwelt in a realm of Thought; and such thought Power, when rightly implemented, can penetrate the dense plane which is the world of human habitation. I did not feel that I had really gone away into a far country. . . . I could still keep in touch. . . .

With this blessed feeling of consolation I must have drifted again, or slipped into a state of passivity.

My next experience came with a strong thought—Exeter!

Again, I was with you in spirit, in the vast Cathedral where the small gathering to remember me was almost swallowed up in the big empty building. This time I was less emotional. I was able to participate in an objective way. My mind could apprehend the order of service. . . . I felt humbled as never before by the kindliness of the souls gathered in that chapel, by the excellently thought-out oration of Colonel Lester, by the constructive 'aura' of the prayer forms as well as by the expressed faith of that Memorial Service.

This is a change you will all make (some very soon), I recall thinking, and then Truth will become apparent. How I longed to materialise before you to show there is no death; but that was beyond my power to do. . . .

By the time the London Memorial Service was held I had 'progressed' sufficiently in this method of extension of consciousness to be able to make my presence known to those who could open their minds to this new dimension of thought. I felt that certain present 'saw' me or were 'aware' of my presence with the Sisters. To me this was uplifting and comforting. . . .

I relaxed into peace. Life goes on for me now on a fuller and more abundant scale of living. . . .

12th December

. . . I am remaining in the Rest Home, though I am now occupying a 'cottage' of my own. It is a lovely peaceful little place, with a very pretty garden (more about this presently).

I still belong to the Home of course, and I go back there frequently. I have been having long talks with Mother Florence, and with Sister Mary and Sister Hilda. They explain this new adventure to me. For this *is* an adventure; that is how I feel about the new life I am now living. It is an adventure . . . probably not permanent . . . for nothing is permanent, not even here! But it is truly stimulating and very satisfying.

This can be described as a 'stretching of the mind' period.

Do you remember how, in the last years, we used to talk and talk, threshing out points of experience; discussing and planning future work? This was, usually I recall, on a Sunday morning over the 'coking-up' of our old boiler. Well, then, we were both on the outside of experience . . . looking inwards. Now the process has been reversed. I am on the inside, looking outwards.

I still have the same experiences, the same problems, the

same hopes, with even greater and wider aspirations for work; only now I view them from an entirely different angle and with far greater dawning comprehension.

Now I am learning to apprehend the meaning of much that happened to me. I see it as a background Pattern. In a way I am beginning to realise the effects of my thoughts and to view the events that were set in motion by these very thoughts and ideas.

This is indeed a most sobering exercise.

When in the body one is so limited by environment, emotions, difficulties, that it is very hard to judge accurately such results as might possibly ensue from the planning, and when we do try to assess the value, we are so often wrong, because we ourselves (our small egotistic selves) get in the way and deflect the Purpose.

Here we live so much more in the realm of mind. As we ponder over an experience or a Purpose, the mind stretches out to see *all* sides of the problem. This is a new and not always exciting or pleasant experience. It is rather like a chain reaction; much more potent and real than the old association of ideas of earth psychology. Here, as one thinks . . . one *is*. I'll try to make this clearer.

There is no compulsion, of course, to review one's past life on earth as soon as one arrives and the new life here begins. Some take a long while to tackle the problem. They dread to see the *effects* of mistakes and failures. . . .

Some of our patients here have got 'stuck'. And that is where I, who myself am undergoing this kind of mental and spiritual 'psychiatry' am able to help them. That is partly why I have elected to stay on here for a space. I shall stay until my own course has become clear (both past and possible future) and until I have been able to rectify the places in the chain where I have failed. My experiences as a teacher, a religious, a psychologist and an earnest seeker after the spiritual life are of great value now. I have some background on which to draw and which might (and sometimes does) help those who are too timid, or frightened, or guilt-ridden, to attempt the work for themselves. Besides, you know the old adage (you are a teacher) that *you learn by teaching.* I'm doing just that now.

The *method* here is interesting and provocative.

33

Somewhere in the deeps of my mind two 'blueprints' are brought forward into my consciousness. These are so clear that I can (literally) take them out, materialise them and study them. One is the Perfect Idea with which my spirit went bravely into incarnation. The other is the resultant of only a partially-understood Plan . . . in fact my life as it was actually lived.

It was a shock to me, and a very salutary experience, to find that these two plans differed exceedingly. And yet, one learns so much by facing the results. . . .

In a way the blueprints resemble maps, with coloured places, and light and dark patches, and a kind of glowing 'sun' for the high-lights. First of all the mind looks at the whole comparison, and sets the blueprints side by side. This is the first shock; a true humbling of yourself to find that you did so little when you would have done so much; that you went wrong so often when you were sure that you were right.

During this experience the whole cycle of your life-term unfolds before you in a kaleidoscopic series of pictures. During this crisis one seems to be entirely *alone*. Yours is the judgment. You stand at your own bar of judgment. You make your own decisions. You take your own blame. . . . You are the accused, the judge and the jury.

This is where quite a few souls in this Rest Home have become immobilised. Their pictures were too searing in their exposures. So we try to help them along, but only when they have made the 'inner desire' to right their wrongs. Until that decision I do not know what happens to them, but I should think that they are 'prisoners of the self'.

Immediately they become ready to face themselves again they are guided to these beautiful and peaceful homes. Here, the Sisters devote their love and thought, their skill and experience, to aiding the 'stumblers'.

The second stage of this recapitulation starts when the soul feels strong enough and calmed sufficiently to take the earth life, round by round (so to speak). Then the blueprints are brought into the mind again; only this time the start is made from the moment of departure from the body. The mind works slowly, oh! so slowly, backwards through one's experiences. (I am not confessing where I have reached in this exercise!) But I will tell you that now you seem *no longer alone*.

34

'Someone' is beside you. Whether it is your own High Spirit or a Great Helper I have yet to discover. Only now, as you ponder, work out, go over, tabulate and judge what you did AND WHY AND WHAT WERE THE RESULTS (good or bad) you are gloriously 'aware' of this great Being beside you, giving strength, peace, tranquillity and helping with constructive criticism. This is a wonderful experience, though harrowing at times. But very cleansing and bringing new hope.

Lots of those here have got 'stuck' on their 'first picture'. So we (the Sisters here in the Home) try to link up with these great ones and bring help and strength to the stumblers' level. Mother Florence is marvellous at this. She has a real technique and this technique is what I am trying, not exactly to copy, but to adapt to my own particular methods of work.

I must tell you about my garden. Yes, it is quite lovely. *And* I still do gardening! Oh, not in the same way as when you used to look at me on my knees grubbing at the soil and say to yourself "There she is again; she shouldn't be doing it!" No. I still go on my knees, but in a different way and not to grub in the soil! (That has a double meaning! . . .)

There is a little patch in my garden which is bright with golden flowers. Do you remember the yellow escholtzia which used to flame all along the border in my garden at Addington? . . . Well, I have a corner of flowers (not escholtzia) but of the same type, golden and glowing. At least, they do not always 'glow'. I have to keep them glowing by 'gardening'. That is, I pour Light and Love into them and over them, rather in the same manner as watering and nourishing them; and they answer (or respond) by growing profusely and gloriously golden.

You remember the 'Secret Place' of our meditations? I call this golden patch my 'secret garden' and some of the patients (those who are trying to become unstuck on their first exercise of recapitulation) come and visit me. We talk and then I guide them to my golden garden, and there they lie and relax and 'tune in' to the higher thoughts of the Great Ones. . . . I thrill when I see some of the results.

There was one man in the wards. He had been brutal and bitter to his wife and family. Now he is stuck. He has spent a long period of your earth time (though there is no time as such over here), since his changeover to this life, in being tied to the places and the people where his cruelty and his bitterness had been exercised.

Now he is here, and is trying to go on. But the film reel of his life appalled him; and he has become completely immobile. He visits me and we talk and talk (rather as I was able to do with some of the prisoners at Maidstone Gaol). Last visit I introduced him to my secret garden. He began to relax. I could *see* it. Some of the imprisoning aura of fear and remorse began to melt away. He lay there amidst that golden light for a very long time and when I did go out to him he smiled. It was the first sign of lightness I have seen in him. He said "Oh, Sister, I feel so much better. Can I come to your garden again?"

You see how this work is done!

It helps me and it helps others. Because this plane is only a few rungs or so higher than the earth plane, there are the same conditions, hospitals, as with your civilisations, and prisons, only here they are selfmade.

I will come again and talk. Bless you.

18th December

No. I did not want to leave the earthly life. I felt that my work had not finished. I tried hard to ignore the deterioration of the body and I prayed to be allowed to remain for some years longer to accomplish the plans for spreading such knowledge as I had gained, amongst others.

But I am content now.

Again, I have been studying the 'Blueprint' of these last years in the light of this new understanding with which I am learning to review the past. This new angle of approach, which is a deeper understanding, has been fostered in my mind (I still have a mind—thank God!), partly by this new freedom from the demands of the body, the emotions, and the pressing of others upon my will; but partly by the wise counsels of dear Mother Florence, of my Sisters and of Father Joseph. Sometimes we have a 'round-table conference' here (rather like a council meeting) and then I put all the questions that bother me to wiser minds than mine. Always I receive answers that fully explain, even though I sometimes have to rationalise the meanings to my own particular conception.

This is a slow process. I progress slowly. But then you know that I had that kind of a mind, which ever needed to read and read, and seek and seek, and absorb and absorb; and even then to rationalise the knowledge gained to my own satisfaction.

Believe me, I did not 'jump out' from the community in which I was professed until after I had sifted and digested the evidence for deeper stratas of psychic and spiritual needs. It took me months of study then, reading and meditation, to make up my mind to such a drastic step. Now, looking back, I see the pattern clearly. I do not regret it. Here all is understood and judged on a wider basis. This is no longer a narrow denominational community. This is a wide and willing service . . . and all is understood and viewed with compassion.

I am exactly the same person now. I still have to go over and over again in my mind the possibilities I had when on earth, the failures and mistakes I made, in the light of this new approach. I still baulk at admitting much that was, perhaps, reprehensible, and which could have been managed without my human bungling. . . .

But here one does not waste effort in regretting blindly. There is too much to learn in a positive manner and to apply to one's future progress. And always there are souls in far worse predicaments from whom lessons can be learned.

I speak of the patients here.

I said we had all grades and classes in the Home—illiterate, uneducated, educated and cultured, rather as I had to teach when I worked as a Tutor-Organiser in the Maidstone prison experiment. Only those were prisoners of the State; segregated from their fellows by rule and power. Here no one is kept against his will or desire. Mostly the patients are happy enough and wish to stay in this temporary security. They cannot move on until they have (literally) seen the Light, or at least as much of the Light as they can assimilate at their present stages. . . .

There is a medical man here. He has been with the Sisters for some space; a brilliant man; alas, he was a drug addict. (But more of him later.)

Generally speaking the dwellers here are of all types; some advanced in many ways, who are literally 'passing through' the Spheres.

Perhaps you will be interested in my latest contact. (I can

37

scarcely call him a pupil, for on earth he was a distinguished scientist!) This man has not long arrived here, from another sphere, and Mother Florence suggested that we talk together. He has a very fine mind, exact and logical, as befits a scientist, of course. It is a mental thrill for me to talk with him. But he was on earth a complete agnostic . . . even an atheist; although he tells me that always his researches came back to the point that there must be a certain X factor which was beyond man's conception, the perfect Creative Factor, a Supreme Mind. Yet in all his work he would not allow that this could be a sign that Life was a matter of progressing consciousness. Indeed, although he has explained to me the wonderful pattern and energy inherent in every atom of matter, and admitted that each atom has a certain measure of consciousness, yet never did he apply this to man himself in the possibility of survival. His thesis was that such consciousness was inherent in the particles of matter and remained as such for the varying type of work for which these atoms were grouped. His theory was (and still is) that the *grouping* of the atoms and cells fixed their effect. Their rotation at certain *rates* of vibration determined the density. Therefore, by changing the *patterns* and *varying* the *vibrations* man could produce differing results. And that was what he was doing; exploring the possibilities of changing the patterns and producing finer (or less dense) types of matter.

This, of course, is exactly what progress means for earth life enlightening the particles of matter into less density.

Only now we have talked together and agreed that this X factor is actually and eternally the Light of Creative Force; and we came to the thrilling conclusion that the scientists' attempt at changing the vibratory rate of atomic matter is the same as all the ancient teaching of the Light permeating the density of man's immersion in matter. If man could keep the Divine Light in mind (which, when out of the prison of the body we can realise as the Permanent Life), man has the power to transform those particles into a finer vibration. The difficulty is that, when we are bombarded by the consciousness of the denser vibrations which make up our bodies, and all the so-called matter of the material world, the Light Eternal is doused and dimmed, sometimes being extinguished altogether.

It has been a wonderful experience, discussion with this man. He sees now that *consciousness* is the expanding X Factor which goes on becoming stronger and more able to lighten matter; and that before him lies a glorious conception of a Universe of ever-increasing Light and therefore, ever-lightening matter with which to experiment.

Now he is absorbed in the wonder, not only that he himself is a unit of consciousness, but also because of his transition from the body, the *pattern* of his own energy ratio has changed, has become less dense, so that he is now able to work at a stepped-up intensity, using a wider field of magnetic force.

What a lot I have learned from him!

Here are two of us conferring; he with his great knowledge of atomic reactions in matter and I, with my inherent conviction that the Spirit is the Light (the X Factor) which is the focus, the power and motive of and for all.

You can understand how thrilling and exciting this is.

My friend (I will call him Mr. M.) will not be here in this Rest Home much longer . . . (I could say 'unfortunately' for I shall miss our sessions). He will be going on to join a group of scientists working on the higher Planes. But he says that he will still make contact with me, even though I elect to stay on here for awhile. And, of course, there is telepathy of the mind for us to radio ideas to each other.

He has much enjoyed the peace of my garden whilst going through the purgation of his concrete mind, and we have had exciting experiments with meditation and also with light transmission to my plants and flowers, being able to observe the results immediately.

"There's your X Factor," I said to him once, with my old enthusiasm. "Look how the Light of Love and Beauty has transformed those flowers into the glowing blossoms they now are!"

"Yes," he said with the characteristic little shake of the head which always comes when he has tabulated a result. "Yes. If only we had been able to realise that Cause and Effect when we were on earth."

"But we will." I felt suddenly illumined. "Your researches in the next Plane will be able to help the earth dwellers to know."

"By telepathy, you mean?"

"By telepathy" I agreed.

And here I am already reaching you on earth about it!

But this is only a taste of that which he, and the scientists he is about to join, will be able to transmit through advanced minds now coming into incarnation on the earth plane for the coming Age.

This is thrilling and soul-satisfying work here. I realise how blessed I am to be able to contact such advanced minds, and to be enabled to transmit my experiences and adventures for those on earth to read, so that they may anticipate with spiritual joy the fullness of Life to come.

An hour or so later

I have realised that you have been going over all this in your mind, and here is the partial answer to the questions you have been formulating.

I said to Mr. M. after a fascinating discourse on protons and electrons and points of bombardment and racial patterns, etc., "So now you see that consciousness is on an upward spiral, and progresses onwards . . . *even your own*, How do you feel about it now?"

He grinned. "I always accept facts" he said "and this is a fact, isn't it? I think. I reason. I learn . . . in fact, I *still am*. One can't dispute facts. . . ."

"Some people called the earth life a great illusion," I persisted. "This could also be an illusion!"

He shook his head.

"I can't accept that earth was an illusion. I was *there*, solid enough to our senses. It was certainly the result of a specific rate of vibration. So if you want to say that this rate of vibration was only the *perception* of substance by the state of consciousness of our brain-minds, I'll agree to that. A projection of our limited minds maybe, but not an illusion. We created our surroundings. . . ."

"What created?" I asked.

"Thought."

"And your X Factor?"

"Still thought, Sister. But of varying vibration and density."

"So that using more X Factor, you'd get a quicker rate of vibration?"

"And a finer type of thought creation."

He gave his characteristic headshake.

"Of course! Now I've got it from your angle. More Light. A wider conception. We *had* all that Light all the time . . . and so few of us knew it!"

"The Churches and all the Religions of the world knew it," I protested.

"Maybe. But I was a scientist. They were building up a theory which nobody had proved."

"And now?"

"Now I've proved one thing . . . I, as a mind, and with a lighter body *survive*."

"But you've proved, partially, the characteristic of the X Factor."

Again he demurred.

"I haven't *proved* it . . . yet, Sister. I've seen it appear to work in our experiments. But I do feel that I am at the beginning of a very exciting quest, instead of at the end of all my researches which I had expected. And that is enough for the moment. . . ."

You see *how* this purgatorial experience works? We don't alter fundamentally. But bit by bit, we move *away* from earth ideas and limitations, and advance more into Light and Wisdom.

1st January 1966

I told you that I would relate my experiences with, and the story of, this brilliant surgeon who is here with us and who, in his lifetime, indulged in drug-taking until it became an addiction. This man has a brilliant mind. On earth he was renowned for the skill of his hands and brain in certain physical operations. (I will not tell you what part of the human body he made his special study, as that might reveal his identity. And here we preserve as much anonymity of our physical life as we can.) His skill was a legend in certain medical quarters. But he became a drug addict, unreliable and uncertain. His health broke and here he is with us in the new Life.

He is a striking looking man, for now he is recapturing the

41

enthusiasm and dedication of his youth, and consequently his body has moulded itself with all the strength and vigour of a young man. He has deep-set eyes and a fine head (leonine you would say in your astrological terms!) and long, sensitive fingers. To have seen those hands and fingers manipulating scalpels must have been a wonderful and moving experience.

But to his story—as he told it to me:

"It all started with an unfortunate affair that came about at a certain period of my life . . . my early forties. There had been trouble in my domestic affairs and I had fallen in love with a very beautiful but heartless woman, who intended to smash my homelife—and did!

"During this period of emotional upset and turbulence I had the terrible misfortune to lose a patient during an operation. To be absolutely honest (and one can be nothing else here) the knife slipped and cut into a vein. The operation had to be suspended whilst this was attended to and the patient's heart failed. In lay circles this was treated as an unfortunate accident; in medical circles my colleagues assured me that the dead man's heart would never have stood the length and severity of the operation anyhow.

"But I knew better. I had not been in my 'real' state . . . in that state in which I performed all my operations. . . .

"Since I was a young man I had always known that the 'surgeon' was within me . . . not I, but this all-knowing, all-perfect someone who, when I stood aside and let Him take over, performed miracles of surgery through my brain and hands. I had made it a practice to keep quiet and be alone for awhile on the days when such skill was required in the course of my work, so as to contact Him. I was never a religious man. I don't think I regarded Him as God or Christ. But He was the strength and the cunning of my hands. His was the inspiration which guided and governed my brain. I was perfectly sure and certain of that, although I never spoke of it to others. Without Him and His judgment, skill and serenity, I was as nothing. And when each operation was over and I went to the tap to wash up, I used to feel physically sick at the possibility that, one day, I might lose touch with Him. . . . I recall I always said 'thank you' after each extended session in the operating-theatre.

"But on this particular day when the accident occurred, I had rushed to the hospital after an emotional row with the woman I thought I loved. There had been no time for quiet, or for recollection of my 'Celestial Surgeon' if I may call Him this. I was in an emotional turmoil.

"After the patient had died and been taken away, I went to the Sister's office and collapsed. Whatever anyone said, *I knew.* I had lost touch with the Inner One. I was desolate.

"I remember that the hospital authorities insisted that I take a holiday. I went to Sicily for three weeks, returning calm in mind and with hope renewed.

"But back in the rush and tension of a surgeon's life something new now reared itself in my mind. *I became afraid.* I tortured myself that perhaps the Inner Surgeon would not be 'there' to guide and help me. I became a soul torn apart, tortured, terrified and almost impotent with the fear and dread that what had happened once might happen again. . . . You see, Sister, I had no knowledge or experience of 'tuning in' to reach this great Inner Spirit, as I am being taught now. Had I realised then that He is (as Christ instructed us) ever ready to be contacted, I might have had strength to go on without making the muddle I did of my life. . . .

"But to resume. I could see (and others warned me) that I was heading for a nervous breakdown. I began to take sleeping-drugs to nullify those long terrifying hours of the night when fear takes hold of the brain. And then a similar operation was presented to me. Life is always like that, I have learned, the rope of one's character has to be tested at its weakest part.

"When I examined the man who was to become my patient, the knowledge went like an electric shock through me. This was an exact replica of the operation which had been so disastrous only six months earlier, a very specialised, very delicate, cutting away of diseased tissue from a most vital part of the human body.

"I went to pieces utterly. To save a lot of painful explanation, I took a drug which I knew would clear my brain, and numb the persistent nagging fears to which I had allowed myself to succumb.

"It worked. I was calm and efficient. I thought I contacted the Surgeon. The operation was entirely successful.

"But that was to be my Achilles' heel. I began to *rely* on the effect of the drug. It seemed to separate away my personal self with all its fears of failure and inadequacy so that the Inner One became the surgeon as before. More and more I fell into this bog of tranquillity. Deeper and deeper I sank until I could no longer operate without the drug.

"That was my weakness. Only now there was the added torture of realising that weakness. Of knowing that strength had left me. I was becoming more and more addicted to this 'outside' stimulation to calm the personal self, and, God help me, I *dare* not give up for fear of being left entirely alone.

"I went on for nearly ten years like this. Oh, yes, I performed some remarkable operations. True. But they were the Inner Surgeon's triumphs, not mine. I was becoming but a poor shell of a man and without medication, neither my brain nor my body would obey me. If there is hell on earth, that was it. Progressively I became the slave of the drugs (now more than one) which I was taking. My mind was in agony; my body attacked by disease and my soul was lost, alone and frightened.

"You know the rest, Sister. My mind broke. I was certified as unsound, put away into a home and there, at length, I was relieved of the diseased body and the illusions of the earth brain.

"And now? . . ."

[Frances speaks]

I was much moved by his story, as we all were. He has had long talks with Mother Florence, with dear Father Joseph, and he has sat in quiet meditation with me, here in my golden garden.

But now I must tell you of the wonderful experience which has 'released' him from wrong judgment, blame and remorse. I was allowed to participate in this experience. . . .

With Mother Florence and Sister Hilda I went to the operating-theatre' as we call it here. (Of course, this hasn't the same connotation as on earth.) Doctor X was already there in the care of Father Joseph. The 'room' if you could call it such, is a long rectangle with a kind of domed ceiling that gives the impression of unlimited space. We sat facing a vista of blueness which appeared to shimmer. There is no wall, just a deep cerulean blue space. I seemed to hear singing, though there is no organ or choir, but there was a faint music of the spheres which is quite indescribable; so soothing that one's spirit rises to float out and participate in the sound.

Suddenly, without preamble, this blue vista broke up, and became a cinema or television screen. Pictures began to emerge on it. They were not superimposed as in a cinema, but seemed to 'grow into it' from the very ether itself. *These pictures appeared to form themselves.*

They showed moments of stress, moments of triumph, moments of failure in the earth life of Doctor X. We saw patients; we watched him in his diagnoses; we followed him to the theatre and witnessed his operations, and as we watched, we became conscious (as he did) of the great Light that enfolded him as he worked.

Light! How much I am learning of the meaning of that word here! How deeply I am beginning to realise the depth of those words 'Light which lighteth every man that cometh into the world'. How paltry is our conception and understanding of that Light! . . . But we will talk of this more, when I have learned and experienced more.

The pictures on the 'screen' went on and on. We were taken into the homes, lives, families of those on whom the Doctor had performed his successful operations. We saw the benefit to humanity, the healings, the resumption of happy, useful lives which were the results of this man's skill. Even when he was working under the influence of drugs (as he said) we were allowed to view the results of what he had accomplished.

I was more than moved; I felt wrung with compassion and a new understanding. Here was a man, standing before the bar of his own judgment, and the scales were showing the balancing up of his actions, and the resulting effects of his service. And when we were shown the skill and success with which he brought a great musician back to health and strength, the scales seemed almost to balance. That musician (now in the Halls of Music in the Spheres) was enabled to go on and leave the world the richer and more exalted by his performances, to add his portion to the beauty that penetrates the materialism of earth-thinking; to lighten, with glorious sound, that darkness into which men sink, and to uplift their spirits in thankfulness to the Creator.

As the film of his life unwound before us, the Doctor saw

45

(though he could scarcely credit it) that he had indeed done his part. He had followed his Pattern, worked out his Blueprint, even though he had badly smudged it in the performance.

At the end he saw! He understood.

His fault had been a weakness in the *soul's* contact with the *personality* which he had allowed to widen until it threatened to break completely. But he had been released before that had happened. His failure had been his refusal to *delve into* that Inner One whom he knew; to contact Him deliberately and reverently at times other than when the 'Celestial Surgeon's' skill was needed. The Light had been within him and about him and he had comprehended it not. . . .

If I should say that there were tears in his eyes when the revelation ended, I would be partly right. *There were tears in his soul*; tears for lost opportunities. But also tears of relief.

I am indeed learning that we must not judge from our very partial understanding. This man, failure as he had seemed, had achieved much. He had been a 'channel of Light' even though he had tried to ignore the implications of this, and even despite the fact that his personality had sunk into a bog of illusions.

Doctor X is a soul with dedicated skill. He will go on to the greater Light, there perhaps to realise his 'Celestial Surgeon' more fully, more potently and intimately and to become united with Him for future service.

Judge not . . . but judge righteous judgment.

But how can we learn to understand, not only people, but more of the great Plan and Pattern for each of us and for humanity? As I am allowed to witness and to assist those souls who gather here for a space, I gain knowledge and a very partial understanding of that Plan and this brings a deep humility, together with a reverence for the wonder and marvel of the Divine Creative Thought.

We went quietly back to our duties leaving Doctor X in the competent care of Father Joseph.

It could almost have been a Christmastide service, as on earth, for truly a new child was born in those who partook of the ceremony. A new compassion and realisation was born in me . . . and a new strength in Doctor X.

As our consciousness expands, we let in more Light. So now

I can really say, with deeper understanding: "Let Light descend on earth!"

3rd January—The Dream

[H.G.]

Two nights after writing the last script, I dreamed of Frances. The dream was strangely haunting, yet vague and indefinite, so that, as I woke to human consciousness, I knew what had happened but the details were hazy.

I had been in a garden which seemed to be set high on a hillside. The strange thing about the garden was that it seemed to be 'etched' in my mind, like a Chinese painting, with a restraint on line so characteristic of eastern art. I remember that there was a single forked apple tree on one side of the garden, but that was all . . . except an impression of space and vista. But the fact that everything was bathed in a soft golden light remained hauntingly with me. I knew that Frances was there with me, and she seemed to appear light and insubstantial, yet we talked together. When I awoke though I could recall nothing of the conversation except what pertained to the closing words "I will carry on from there" which I recall saying.

But exactly what that meant to convey to me, my conscious mind could not, or would not, formulate. (I am very sure though that the Real Self knows and will carry out the promise.)

3rd January

[Frances resumes]

I have become great friends with Doctor X. He and I have long talks on all sorts of subjects. We are both sure that we have had links together in former lives. Yes. He accepts reincarnation. He says that, in his medical work, he had known how marvellous was Nature in her precision, recapitulation and application; that life itself must be in a series. He confesses that the conviction that he had failed in this round haunted the last years of his time on earth.

Now, as you can understand and appreciate, he is eager to go on. He desires to learn, to become strong, to absorb Light, and then return to earth with his innate skill, but with a stronger link and memory of the Spirit, and a true one-ness with his soul. His is a great soul. I find him splendid and stimulating. His is the type of personality which, had I encountered as a young woman, would have intrigued me. He had realisation of his Inner Self. He knew! But now, he groans whenever I point that out, because he feels that his failure was greater than the sin of ignorance; he was not strong enough to hold the contact with which he was cognisant. To me—this is an interesting point. He is an old soul, an advanced ego, and *he knew*.

Many, many people do not even have that consolation of knowing of the Power Within, yet he could not, in his smaller self, maintain the contact. What technique could have helped him to maintain and strengthen it?

The answer is that technique and method which has been known by the few throughout the ages; the technique of communion with the Divine; of using an act of will to close away the illusions of the earth and to open the channel into the Divine Source, into the light of *conscious knowing*.

I tried, in my small way, and possibly quite unconvincingly, to teach on earth the value of meditation periods when the personality gravitates towards the light of the soul and spirit. I failed too, because in some ways I could not surmount my own personal barriers. Here I am learning so much more. I shall go on to talk of meditation and contemplation again later, and on the methods pertaining here. Also (as I am beginning to understand) the actual way in which these techniques work. There is nothing vague or woolly, I assure you. It is, as Mr. M. would have said, entirely a scientific process.

But to proceed.

I went with Doctor X to 'visit' some of his contemporaries and his friends in another part of this new life. I suppose you would call this the higher Planes. I cannot say for sure. Anyway, we found ourselves within a 'medical circle' of souls. There were many souls and they radiated a joyous concentration that was catching. We soon found ourselves chatting away eagerly in groups. One was there who had been a great physician, a beloved physician, when on earth; a soul whose countenance was beautiful beyond any description of mine. He radiated spiritual love and beauty. He appeared to be a Leader of this group. He spoke with Doctor X and I stood beside him, so

48

lifted in thought and inspiration that I felt almost exalted. Yet I knew that I could not bear the High Frequency of His vibration for long. This Leader said that soon He would have the pleasure of welcoming Doctor X on to his 'staff'. I was thrilled for my new (yet old) friend. I was so happy for him. It was a moment, I felt, of supreme achievement.

Then we met the musician whose life on earth Doctor X had been able to prolong by his medical and surgical skill. The musician has promised to take us to the Halls of Music. He wasn't at all my idea of what a musician should be . . . he was gay, almost jolly, and he teased Doctor X.

"So you have brought your nurse?" he asked. (I am still in a habit.)

"Not my nurse," the doctor answered, "my teacher. Sister and I have thrashed out many problems and puzzles together."

"You will be leaving there soon?" asked the musician.

"Not before he has passed the Eleven Plus" I put in, not quite realising what I was saying. Then I wanted to get away, feeling that I had made a gaffe. But they took it in good part.

"Sister is quite right" Doctor X said, "and if this is the junior school work then I can look forward, with great eagerness, to the upper classes."

It was my most marvellous experience of this new aspect of Life. I felt *filled* with Light . . . that is the only way I can express it. But neither of us could hold this great intensity of vibration for long. We felt (so to speak) used up by this High Frequency so that, presently I, for one, had the strange experience of dwindling. And then we were both back in my garden and Sister Hilda was there to tell us that there was an urgent situation arisen in the Home.

But we had both had a taste of the beauty of the Higher Spheres and of communion with progressed souls. . . . I felt as though I was shining. The Light stayed with me.

This is Life . . . Life more abundant.

The same day (3rd January)—later

Sister Hilda and I returned to the Home. Mother Florence awaited us. She took us apart and told us that a new, and very difficult 'patient' had just been brought in. Quietly she told us the facts about this new arrival.

The man had been a Nazi leader; wellknown and extremely powerful during the last war. After the downfall of Germany he had committed suicide. (I cannot give his name but it is not Hitler.) Since that time he had been 'lodged in the shadows'. Mother Florence explained that he had been 'wandering in the lower places'. You would no doubt refer to this dark place as the 'lower astral'. In any case, for twenty earth years, he had been imprisoned by his own evil.

Now he had been rescued. He was conscious of his terrible cruelty and filled with remorse. Mother Florence warned us that he would need very special nursing, care, understanding and help. Also that we might get a shock at his appearance which, I gathered was not a sight such as I had ever witnessed.

Mother also warned us to draw 'a web of protection' around us and to hold firmly to the Light.

I was apprehensive as we went towards a separate ward at the far end of the Home. But not prepared for the sight that met us.

The ward was dark and gloomy, very different from our usual light and sunny rooms. A pall of murky twilight seemed to hover over it. Only slowly did it become apparent to us that 'something' lay on the bed. I looked away quickly from the repellent sight. The poor creature's body appeared to be covered with sores and scars; the eyes were closed.

"He thinks he is blind" Mother Florence whispered. "He is not of course. But the Light here is too bright and penetrating for him as yet; and he cries out that it has blinded him."

The man was a terrible and pathetic sight. As I looked away again I became aware of Father Joseph who sat at the head of the bed behind the patient.

"Now" I heard Father Joseph say, although there was no *apparent* sound in the room. "This poor unfortunate creature needs all our care and compassion. He has come to us to be healed and to be enabled to face himself and judge his deeds when he wakens from his terrible ordeal of darkness. Let us together concentrate our thoughts and blessings on him. Let us *feel* a gentle soft healing Light, God's healing Force of the utmost sweetness and gentleness pour out from our souls to his.

Let us ask that Light may come into this place; that it may touch him, comfort him and give him sweet sleep. . . ."

I looked round swiftly. There were Father Joseph, Mother Florence, Sister Hilda, Sister Cecilia and myself. They looked utterly calm. Slowly, as I sank deeper into concentration, I felt myself swept up into a great joy and strength and power. The poor creature moaned but I scarcely heard him. The ward had been dark. Gradually Light grew in it; in one corner an intense shimmer of Light became clearly visible; a Light that condensed into a white-hot Flame, like a pillar of fire.

Then I knew that a Celestial Being had added His Ray of Spirit Force. I found myself praying, not only for this tormented soul but also for the souls of his victims.

Suddenly, in the midst of my prayers, I was 'transported' back into the Community Chapel in South Africa. I *heard* the Sisters singing, and I joined in:

Unto us a Child is born,
Unto us a Son is given . . .

The hymn swelled. I was *there*, with the Community, singing, yet I knelt here by the bedside of this lost, broken soul. I started because I felt that I must have been singing aloud; but no one moved. Then a Voice echoed in my mind . . . and the words were similar to those of the Master Jesus.

"Father, forgive him. He knew not what he did . . ."

I found myself on my knees gazing at the Light, now slowly diminishing. It was an awareness so wonderful, and so shattering that I felt my whole self tremble.

At that moment I had been *at one* with the Sisters on earth in their prayers and intercessions for 'all sorts and conditions of mankind', as well as *at one* with this small band of dedicated and devoted Servers of the Light; and at the same moment *at one* with the penetrating white Light of a great healing Angel.

There is no separation. We are all one.

"Neither heaven nor earth nor hell can separate us from the love of God" I murmured to myself as the realisation flooded me that the patient had literally come from hell to us. . . .

The great Light faded slowly, but now the gloom had gone from the ward. Our patient lay still. The rigours of his body had ceased. He seemed to be asleep.

51

"In the next ward", Mother Florence was saying, "is a woman who was one of his victims, a young Jewish mother who has arrived with him. She has been bound to him by her deep hatred. But she is progressing because she had real love in her heart for her husband and child who were snatched from her. She has the power of Love in her soul. He, poor creature has not . . . yet. . . ."

"And", Mother Florence went on, "when he is healed sufficiently they must confront one another and learn forgiveness, understanding and charity."

I was aware then that Father Joseph had slipped away. Mother Florence also left us and the three of us remained behind to keep vigil.

> *Unto us a Child is given,*
> *Unto us a Son is born . . .*

rang in my mind. The Christmas hymn seemed out of context. Yet the thought persisted in my mind: "This *is* a beginning, a birth. This is a new life being born, a soul being brought into Light." Slowly I seemed to melt into an all-embracing meditation and contemplation upon God's Peace and Light; a depth of contemplation such as I had never before known. It was a most truly wonderful experience.

At last, it seemed, I had 'broken through' that barrier which throughout the entire period of my earthly life, had barred my way.

Of such a Peace I cannot speak, for words cannot express it.

But enough if I say, with all sincerity, that I felt I truly understood at last the meaning of those words "My Peace I give unto you. Not as the world gives, give I unto you. . . ."

I had found a new measure, a new capacity, and I was awake in the Light. I was carried in that peace to my own cottage where, later, I found myself.

Our patient still sleeps. . . .

5th January

I have been to visit the 'medical group' again with Doctor X. It is the name by which I call the Group though I am sure that they have a more exalted title. I did not meet the Leader of their Group again. Maybe, as a very new girl, I have to learn to tune up my vibrations to meet Him. (This is merely a surmise on my part from the last experience. Nobody has informed me of this.)

You were correct in your idea about Him. He is a very advanced soul, a Master in His own right, and disciple of the Lord Jesus who, I have been told, lives in a Plane far beyond this. (On this subject I must stress that so much of the old theology of the Christian Churches is at fault. It must be a rare occurrence, I imagine, for any newly-arrived soul in this world to find himself 'at rest in the arms of Jesus'. Not because of any lack of devotion, nor because Jesus is unaware of the soul's discipleship, but from the more practical standpoint it is only reasonable that souls must take into account the differences . . . and these are *vital* . . . in frequencies of vibration. No soul coming here from earth's limitations, however advanced it may be in spiritual truth, is able to stand the stepped-up vibrations or the translucent Light of these High Planes. It appears from my observation during my time here, that one has to earn every step of advancement. Did not the Master Himself take three days before, as He said "I ascend to my Father?" These cryptic words are much more understandable and translatable even from this plane of the Astral than they could possibly be from the earth level consciousness.)

Perhaps, because at my previous visit when I was blessed enough to meet this great physician I felt 'used up' and of a quite inadequate vibration to raise myself to the penetrating power of His Light, another contact has not been permitted. Though I shall ever remember the beauty and love and light in His face and the dazzling luminous robe that He wore.

Those of His Group told me that the Leader (it is easy to feel their reverence and respect for Him), is not always with them. To our earthly way of thinking, which has not yet left me, He fulfills the role of Director of their work and study. He visits them, it seems, when there is a new impulse in their researches to be studied and tested or, as in the case of Doctor X, when a new boy, so to speak, was to be interviewed and judged ready for admission.

He is an inhabitant of Planes beyond any of this medical fraternity in the Priority A Group. . . .

Doctor X revelled in talking with his old associates, and with legendary figures of importance in the medical profession. Lister was amongst them. I was able to have a word or two with Pierre Curie, even though on earth he was a Frenchman and my French was never fluent. Language affords no difficulty over here; and I yet do not know if I spoke in French or he in English. Or even if, in the earthly sense we 'spoke' at all!

He referred to the sad prostitution of the usefulness of the atom and its power. Mankind is poisoning not only the earth on which these particles of atomic dust settle, but the atmosphere itself; the envelope of the earth sphere, as well as herbage and animal, bird and human life.

I asked him if he now regretted his life work. He shook his head.

"Not at all. Progress must always present a dark and a light side to those who live almost entirely in the gloom of a slow inert vibration. Our work is to try to enlighten the vibrations of the earth plane so that these oppositions are not allowed to *continue to act* in negative ways. There can be no comparison, of course, between the ignorant mind, which was ready to fight for his belief that his world was square, and the partially-freed mind which *knows*, not only that the earth is a ball of matter that is forever circling, but also that it is merely a conglomeration of atoms held together by a fixed vibratory rate."

Doctor X intervened. "And what about the diseases man is bringing upon his kind through his abuses? And the possibility of complete annihilation by the very method of atomic power for destruction which he has discovered?"

Pierre Curie spread his hands in a gesture of resignation.

"Mankind must progress. It learns slowly and such slow progress with many mistakes brings pain. But if you regard life from the angle of an *eternal process* you get a different feeling about it. The Life Force is not expanded on only one terrestrial globe. Neither is it ended by being precipitated from that globe by what humanity calls death. Here we see a little further along the Eternal Road, but only a *limited* distance. As we learn to purify our vibrations, to enlighten our 'bodies' and thus refine them into the actuality of receiving more Light from the Divine Mind, so we progress onwards. Doors open to us which were closed before; perception grows clearer and keener and we are able to comprehend more fully the true meaning and purpose for which the Life Force has descended into the slowest and most inert vibration."

"And the people of earth?" the Doctor persisted.

"Will return and return after they have made their souls more capable of transmitting this Life Force in order to transmute the density of earth vibration into a higher frequency.

"And disease and destruction?" I asked.

"Man will die, as he has ever done. As long as he believes that death is the end, disease and destruction will last. . . ."

Suddenly I comprehended his meaning. Mankind is using *palliatives*, when the *cure* is within its grasp. Change the *angle* of belief; do away with the dread and fear of death and teach the eternal One-ness of life. That is redemption, both of man and of the earth. This may take thousands of years. But there are millions of years behind us. Man has taken centuries to lift his inert response thus far; but he is on an upward path. Here is the old answer again. Light and yet more Light; Light of understanding, of knowledge, of wisdom and true perception to penetrate this fog of illusion in which the mass of mankind still wanders.

"And you," I ventured to ask Curie, "you work on this progress?"

He smiled. "We are perhaps employed on the palliative side; to relieve and cure that which misapplied thought and energy and ignorance have crystallised. But in its way that is Light too."

We left, much inspired.

More than ever we realised the earth's crying need for light.

Jesus came to show and demonstrate that man lived on after leaving the earth plane. He taught that this God Force, this Life is truly within every one of us, dimmed yet unextinguishable. He was not received by His fellows, yet His Light, that High Frequency of vibration which He was able to transmit to earth, lives on.

The Doctor and I recalled that Invocation which I repeated often when in the body:

> *May Light descend on earth . . .*
> *May Christ return to earth.*

55

I felt that I understood partly the deep meaning of that Invocation now.

8th January

Our 'patient' is still 'sleeping'. He has not changed and possibly will continue to rest in this pure Light of healing and love until his soul has regained sufficient strength and peace to begin its long progress onwards.

I have talked with the Jewish girl who arrived with him. She has recovered sufficiently to begin to re-orient her thought; to change the angle of her thinking. She was a 'good' woman, that is, she was moral and kind and loving, but it will take much instruction and gentle working out of her problems before she will be enabled to view the horror of what happened to her in an objective manner. The old ingrained 'eye for an eye, and tooth for a tooth' belief has to be transmuted through this new angle of judging into an appreciation of Love as the instigator of life. Already some of the virulent hatred is dissolving as she now realises that the avenger receives nothing constructive or worth while by insisting on recompense.

Mother Florence told her about the poor soul who was the instigator of her tragedies, and she knows that he is even now resting, and being 'healed'. So far she can scarcely bear to think of his being healed, but she will. Now all that she asks is to be reunited with the husband and child who were taken from her. Her own sufferings in the camp to which she was taken and where she later died, are being obliterated in her consciousness as she is learning to relax and let go of the earthly life and all the terror and hate in it, and to live in the Light.

Her husband, who was a German lawyer, was 'rounded up' and transported to a labour camp where he too, later, died from injuries and exposures. She never knew what happened to her little girl. Mother Florence tells me that the husband has been 'located'. He did not hold the hatred in his soul so deeply or so bitterly and has progressed more easily. He has awaited the arrival of the wife he loved and has continually sent her Love and Light, even whilst she was sojourning in those shadowy worlds of the lower astral bound by the hate bonds to the man who had caused the tragedies. Perhaps it was the very fact of that Light sent down to her and to the soul of the man who was responsible for the cruelties, which helped to set them free from the underworld, so that Messengers could bring them here. In the nature of consciousness (which is the way here of saying 'in the fullness of time) he will come to meet her. They will be reunited and will go their way together. Of the child I know nothing.

Our scientist Mr. M. has left us. He is not yet ready I understand, to work in the Higher Spheres, or even to join a Band who are connected with Those who work in such a sphere; but he has recovered and become more ready to accept the truths he had rejected on the earth. But he has to make right a lack that was in his personality life, a lack of love. He was always so absorbed in the logical, reasoning mind when on earth that he had no time for the usual feelings for his fellow men. He was frightened of being involved by love, so he never married or felt affection for any woman. He lived entirely for himself and for his work.

Now he has gone to rejoin, for awhile, his mother, father and sisters, and so learn to be part of a family unit. You know that we are all parts of a Family or a Group and if we refused to accept this, either in the fulfillment of family life, group life or community life when on the earth plane, or refused to co-operate unselfishly with such groups when we had the chance, we are held back here from progress until we have made good that lack! So he will join in and practice unselfishness and give freely of his sympathy, love and compassion in service to his companions before he will be allowed to go on and rejoin the scientific research which is his great desire.

For myself I have been going through a sort of 'cleaning out' process, and in this dear Mother Florence has been as helpful, gentle and understanding with me as she was in the months preceding my final Profession into the religious life. She is a wonderful soul and has voluntarily given her service to these her fellow beings in the work of this home. But she 'visits' other Spheres I am certain, although she has never told me so. She goes away from us and when she returns I am certain she is not wearing the usual habit which is her accustomed clothing. Once I met her just as she came back to us, her face was radiant. I was sure then that she was clothed in the 'robe of the Spirit'. It

57

was a deep blue robe of great beauty. Later, without any explanation, she resumed the habit in which she greets our patients. Mother Cecilia is also only with us occasionally. . . .

As for my own 'life' here, I retire more and more to the deep joy and peace and rest of my garden amongst my flowers. You recall that I could never sit and enjoy relaxation in my garden when on earth. I was always too anxious to get on with my jobs.

Over here there is no such urgency.

More and more I am learning to let go of urgency and to let my soul sink deeply and refreshingly into contemplation of the joy of the Spirit.

This develops into what you would call a 'dream-life' yet it is really a stretching out of the soul to a wider consciousness. I revel in Light and peace and a new joy. I cannot describe it more clearly than that.

If I say that now I understand the meaning of the phrase 'Rest in the Lord' that might help. Yet there is no personality about this experience. God is Light, Energy and Joy to me. I rest in that Light and am healed from my many mistakes. And I live a more abundant Life.

11th January

I call him 'the man on a bicycle'. He is a soul who has been here in this Home for a long time by earth standards. He was killed in a bicycle accident, I should imagine, just before, or early in, the First World War because he couldn't recollect anything about any war when I talked with him. Here he is in what I call my psychiatric ward. He was a sneak-thief. He made an art of stealing and he was never caught. He was killed when his bicycle got out of control on a steep hill because the brakes did not act. He ran into the car (one of the early vintage) of a woman he had systematically robbed for years; vegetables from her garden, cash from her house which he had broken and entered. As she was in business in the town where he lived he knew her hours of absence from home. She never suspected him. It seems he was very expert at forcing window-catches and climbing drain-pipes. He worked as a labourer, but he had Ideas! One was that 'all things are free'. He was right of course

58

—in a way. All things should be free and if man had reached such a stage of evolution, so it would be. But man has not. Everything is free here of course. That is one of his stumbling blocks in our long and rather involved talks together.

"It's free here! Why shouldn't it have been free for all there?" he keeps asking.

Can you see our difficulty?

We have to teach him that morally he was wrong, though spiritually the world and its absorption with possessions was wrong too. Only he still refutes the suggestion that he was overwhelmed with the desire for possession! . . .

He is a strange 'locked-up' soul, willing and helpful, but he cannot seem to get past his dogged beliefs, nor to adapt himself to the new life here. He 'works' about the home; his limited intelligence has not even yet realised that he need not go to call the Sisters, or *dig* to plant the flowers. So he goes on his own old way; and we talk to him and try to persuade him to accept this new phase of Life which he has entered. He appears to have become static, and so he may remain until his Higher Self is awakened in him. He is perfectly content with being where he is and is not at all aspiring to anything more Real.

Reality! What is it?

What an illusion thought is! I *thought* I was real enough on earth. Now I realise that what seemed important and substantial and worth while was but a shadow of a shadow! I'm not really Real here! This too is merely the shadow which is but a shell, or covering, of something else. I'm on a journey still . . . perhaps to the Centre, certainly to a higher point, but what this is I scarcely dare imagine. I've only peeled off the outer shadow yet, the outer skin . . . rather like peeling skins from an onion. One goes on shedding; it seems an eternal process.

In my long contemplative times, when the Spirit in me rises and seems to take flight towards the next step, I become uplifted and eager, so very eager, for that succeeding stage. Yet I know that I have to remain where I am and do just what I am doing until I have shed more of the 'shadow-covering'. . . . You know I always wanted to go forward too quickly. Often I visualised happenings an incarnation ahead. Remember how we used to talk? I would envisage great Beings walking with men on earth. That time will come, no doubt. Perhaps is al-

59

ready happening, but men have no vision to see. Now of course I recognise the drawbacks; man would not yet be ready to receive them.

Even in this stage, beyond the physical limitations, our patients would not be able to *believe*, let alone accept, the appearance of Great Ones. I have been blessed indeed, for I have been permitted to meet such a Great One in the Beloved Physician of the Doctors' Group. . . . But then I came here expecting such!

The Planes of the Spirit stretch onward into infinity. What joy it will be, going forwards, gravitating (even though slowly) to one's true Place! I presume each Plane will *seem* real, will have more reality than the preceding one.

That sounds like a paradox!

But reality itself? It is quite beyond our comprehension.

I have talked long with Mother Florence upon this. She is so much further advanced; she seems to pass at will between the Planes. Yet she admits there is so much more, infinitely much more, beyond that to which she is admitted. I *long* to go on, to view those Planes of Light, to touch those Great Lives; yet I am content here and happy. As one must be! You can't *push* yourself into heavens beyond you; the Law of Progression is exact.

But I *am* trying to shed some of the clutter of the personality. We all have to do that. . . . And there are three ways in which to carry it out here. By self-judgment, and true assessment of experiences; by service to one's fellows; and by aspiration.

Not so different, you will say, from the earth life after all!

But oh, with so many, many compensations!

I can express it best in this thought; the 'subjective' of the earth plane mind has become the 'objective' in this new state of Being. This I begin to comprehend, is the law of progress. By it we advance onwards into realms of incredible beauty and wonder. How can I make this clear?

The 'subjective' or inner content of my thoughts, aspirations and desires here and now will fashion the 'objective' place to which I will pass on the next stage of my journey, just as the inner life of the soul within the body-mind on earth decides the first future 'home' on this level.

More and more important therefore and invaluable, is the

inner life of meditation and contemplation and at-one-ment with Divine Beauty and Truth. The saying on earth 'As a man thinks, so is he' is true in essence, truer than our ideas can conceive. By man's thoughts and inspirations he weaves for himself his future place in this dimension. This is logical Law. In the earth life he can build a façade about himself. Here he has no such mask. He is known here for what he is, and for what *his inner subjective* life has made him.

Think then of the importance of Light in the soul. The intensity and power with which Light illumines the inner life are objectified here; the newly transported soul graduates always to its rightful place, to the place it has earned and prepared.

'Lay up for yourselves treasures in heaven' may be taken as having a *factual* meaning.

13th January

We had an 'arrival' who did not stay with us. After a rest she continued on her way. This was an interesting case; this was a woman who had been nurse and missionary for many years of her life in Africa, and had *lived* the Christian religion. She was put to death when there had been an uprising by the natives, and with her, a small native boy whom she had befriended. They had arrived here together, for it seemed that even in the period of transition to this plane she had held the child to her with love.

This is a woman whom (if I had not learned better) I could find within myself to envy. She is such a beautiful soul, with the Light of Love surrounding her like a halo. Her first words, when she became conscious of her surroundings, were "I knew I would wake up amongst Sisters. Thank God! It is wonderful!" There was, in her mind, no question of surviving the terrible ordeal through which she had met death; there were no recriminations, no fears and most impressive of all, no hatreds. She exuded unselfish love.

Her quick concern was for the little dark-skinned boy. When she learned that he was here with her safely 'sleeping' she almost wept with joy.

"You see, I promised his parents who 'went on' some time

61

before, that I would look after him" she said. "Now I can really rest awhile."

She was a joy to us all here—a soul full of light and beauty. She and I had great talks. I told her of my visit to the Doctors and of the Great Physician who is their Leader. She was thrilled and uplifted. I knew that soon she would find herself in the Presence of some great Soul.

"But not before little Laki has been restored to his own parents" she insisted.

So the Sisters set out to find the boy's parents. I do not mean, of course, that they did this in the physical sense in which we would have done it on earth. They 'concentrated', asking for help from the Great Ones who direct the newly-arrived souls. They also sent out their thoughts to contact the 'beam' on whose Ray these souls were abiding. And a contact was made.

A Messenger arrived with a guide, and little Laki went on to his rightful place. His foster-mother was overjoyed for she knew that she would be able to visit him and help him as she had done when in the physical body. Here I must say a word about the boy. A child is so much nearer to the soul-life. Even this child's few short years on earth, six I believe, had scarcely separated him from his before-birth contact with Divine Love. This Love had been continued for him by his missionary 'mother'. He accepted our new life with a quiet wonder and yet a fulfilled joy. He loved us all, and once he told Mother Florence of a great angel whom, he said, he had seen with us in the home. For me it has been a precious and wonderful experience to have witnessed the re-birth here of such innocence; the soul of this child, unpolluted, untainted by the materialism and separation of earth beliefs, was so ready for the heaven world. I can express it best by saying it was like a bud opening into flower here. Please write this and stress it, for it will, I feel, give comfort to those fathers and mothers who may have been separated by what the world calls death from their little ones.

Laki rejoined his people; our missionary rested with us. To me she was a lesson without words! How much I learned from her!

For she was indeed one of the Chosen.

Her brief sojourn with us here helped me to re-think over my old set of values. We do make the mistake of valuing intellect too highly in the earth life, scorning the *simple* follower of Reality. This woman has intelligence but not a trained or well-developed intellect. . . . But she lived daily from the true Centre of herself. In other words, the Spirit was her daily guide and every problem, every difficulty and every joy she took to this Master within. She *radiated* peace and love and joy; and death had meant little to her. She was well acquainted with the Inner Voice and obeyed the Higher Will. It had taken her through strange experiences; yet it was quite clear that she had brought a Divine Ray into the world with her, lowly and far from clever as she was.

She had *lived* what so many of us had *talked* about.

The values are awry on earth. Intellect and a trained brain-mind are great adjuncts, but they often become barriers to truth and a true expression of Divine Love. Man's reasoning mind must learn to be obedient to and co-operative with the Inner Self, the Christ in every man of the teaching of the Master Jesus, and the Light within of eastern sages. To me, this has been demonstrated very clearly by the 'passing through' our Station of this great soul so simple yet profound in her understanding of at-one-ment with truth.

Mother Florence has told me about her departure.

She and our missionary were talking together on the terrace here when Mother Florence observed that her patient appeared to have gone into a deep contemplation. They remained still and silent. Mother felt a great Presence as of an Angel of Light with them; she held her soul in quiet expectation. Then the Light grew stronger about them, the air more potent, and there was a 'feeling' of music' Her missionary friend, she says, impulsively stirred, put out her hand and touched Mother Florence.

"Thank you and bless you all for your kind reception of me" she whispered. "How splendid your work is here! And I realise that it is entirely voluntary. But your true Place is waiting for you all when you have completed your service. May I often come and visit with you?"

Mother Florence felt that she had no words with which to reply except "God bless you."

The Light grew and multiplied about them and Mother said

that her eyes were only able to perceive the Light and nothing more. She felt herself swept upwards into enlightenment.

When her 'spirit returned' (those are *her* words), our missionary had left. She had gone to her rightful Place. Love had been translated to Higher Spheres, you see, long before intellect, as in the scientist, or skill, as with Doctor X had been ready to ascend. What a lesson for us here and for those on earth! Please record it.

13th January—Later

Our Nazi patient is still the same; inert, motionless, shut up in the shell of himself. A shell indeed.

Father Joseph tells me that the poor creature might be like this for what we would say on earth, many years. He has already been held in the dark bondage of the hell of his own making since the end of the last war, and that is over twenty years ago. (I am fast losing count of time as we knew it on earth.) Things 'happen' here; souls or entities at all the lower stages of progress come and go; we either leave or we stay; but we do not reckon these events in time. We live, or we exist, according to the level of our thought-life; some are content to stay, thinking no doubt that this is the final stage. There must, of course, come a time in the soul's awakening when that belief is proved false, but Father Joseph tells me that some souls settle down in one stage for years . . . even centuries! While others persist in their former earth surroundings for ages!

Our Nazi then may lie like this long after many of the patients, helpers and servers here have graduated to Higher Spheres.

Still we have regular 'thought-sessions' for him. Even the Jewish woman has been to see him! She stood looking at this pathetically disfigured soul and at last she whispered: "He doesn't *look* so evil, does he?"

The wonderful lesson about this is that by the time he is ready to confront her, she will have progressed enough to be able to forgive all the injuries for which he was responsible; and she will be prepared to help him. And he will need help!

I talked to our wise Director about this. Father Joseph said that although we are doing all we can, it is a pity that there are no prayers which could be said for the man's soul from the inhabitants of the earth plane. Interested in this point of view I asked for explanations.

"Prayers and good thoughts" he told me "for those who have left the earth life, by their fellows still in incarnation, are a great aid to our work here. The prayer forms, and the potency of good thoughts, cause a quickened vibration to reach the one prayed for. As he is generally closely connected with his former life by interests and affections and memories, he is able to respond to such vibrations; thus he is much helped. Such petitions and meditations could be likened to a draught of healing water for the newly transmitted soul." Our Adviser shook his head with what I felt was infinite sadness. "But alas, there is no one on earth to pray ever for the repose of this poor soul. . . ."

I thought deeply about this.

Poor soul he is . . . but not a 'lost soul'. There must have been some good which the Great Ones recognised, otherwise our Nazi patient would not have been 'rescued'. His besetting sin, which blacked out all else, was love of power; it swelled into viciousness against another race, even causing him to put to death men, women and children of that race. But unless we are All-Wise how can we judge what he did? I have always believed in reincarnation, and have as yet had no cause to believe otherwise; I wonder then, with what provocations and with what bitter soul memories this poor creature hastened back to rebirth! There have been monsters throughout history who have burned, tortured, pillaged and ravaged. What has happened to them? They could not all have been 'lost'. Poor creatures, they must have crawled up out of the slime of their misdeeds into some soul-light at some time, and perhaps then, have hastened back to birth with only half-digested knowledge.

Always, I feel certain, those ahead must have reached down a helping hand, or sent a loving thought, for no soul is left alone. But as each soul must come to the judgment of his earth deeds and results of them, one can only ask for strength to be vouchsafed to this poor, deluded entity when he too stands at the bar of judgment. Will no one on earth pray for his soul at that time?

We have been instructed to 'pray for those who despitefully use us'. Here, surely, is a living example for us all.

Perhaps this is a notorious case. But what of the millions more who, during their short span on earth, have done evil and have paid for their crimes (as we have so smugly said) by execution, and then have been forgotten?

Have no prayers been moulded by Love into thoughts of compassion which could reach them in their darkness? Have we ever remembered them and called for aid for the reckoning of their misdeeds? It is a sobering thought. In such a connection we might discover that our negligence and the self-interest in which we have enclosed ourselves might call for recompense when we reach this world.

You ask about Rescue Circles?

When I was in the body I knew about this method of help and even attended such groups myself, when I was investigating. But the investigators and helpers must be very pure in heart and very sure of Divine Help and Strength when attempting such work. Now that I have witnessed, for myself, the state of such a soul from outer darkness, I am aware more potently of the dangers of such groups, and would advise caution.

Yet the sending out of Light from the Centre by groups at meditation times, the deliberate formation of a prayer thought to reach down and touch those poor benighted ones, a moment of remembrance in a holy place, even the uttering of the names of such unfortunates, commending them to Divine Mercy . . . all are helps towards the resurrection of those who dwell in darkness.

Forgive me if I have preached; such is not my wish. I can only trust that the describing of my grave experiences here may bring some echo of compassion into the hearts of those who read.

15th January

I have met my family, and visited my father, mother, sister and brother. But as this is a private affair and not relevant to the purpose of these communications, I shall not write about it. . . .

Our Nazi patient still sleeps. His Jewish victim has been visited by her husband, a kind and gentle soul, and they have talked long and earnestly. The child, who was taken from her, is not, it appears, in this World. Her husband told of his long

66

search. At last he was told that the child had lived on and had grown up. Poor soul she exists, bitter and unhappy and sunk into a sordid life.

On learning this information, the mother at first reverted to her bitterness and longing for revenge but, as Father Joseph and her husband pointed out to her, revenge has no meaning now. There is no avenging of injury either here, or I imagine, in the realms above; there is only understanding, forgiveness and selfless love.

After much discussion (and I was 'called in' to speak at some of the sessions) our poor sad mother became calmed and was enabled to see Purpose in all things. Now she is as anxious as her husband to locate the girl and get into touch with her by thought, love and concentrated prayer. She herself needs a great deal more cleansing of her 'etheric' before she can succeed in her quest. But she is already a different soul. The old hard shell is melting from her. Gentleness and maternal love shine in her. She is happy to be once more with the husband she lost, and is preparing to join him in the home he is preparing for her. At first she may sojourn with him for a space, returning here to rest and grow strong in her soul. Later, when the healing is accomplished, the way will be open for these two souls to be together, and to contact their daughter. . . . I mean that the Powers-that-be who operate these contacts from this side will find a 'channel' through which the girl may be reached, Light and Love will be poured upon her. . . .

Our Doctor X has made many visits to his medical fraternity. He returns to us filled with new hope, new eagerness to proceed with his progress and his future work. From his last visit he came to me, shining with happiness.

"It's wonderful, Sister" he burst out "I've learned so much. Why, oh why, couldn't I have known of this when I lived on earth? What a marvellous Purpose and Plan there is to Life! And how small, almost insignificant, the struggles, fallacies and failures of the last earth life appear now."

I urged him to go on and to tell me more of his discoveries.

He is thrilled, he admits, with the prospect of future work and research. He sees how this devoted Band of medical men under their Teacher and Leader are fast finding ways of relieving humanity of some of its suffering.

"We are still only on the palliative side, as Curie puts it" he said "for man must be allowed to go on and use his discoveries for destruction and for evoking fear and submission in his fellows until he learns better. But meanwhile the Band is helping to 'put through' ideas on the origin and treatment of disease. . . ."

"Cancer?" I asked, remembering (now with only a slight shudder of distaste) the ravaging of my own earth body.

"Yes. Cancer." He nodded. "We were discussing how this disease is caused in the first instance, by one cell going 'berserk', becoming a rogue cell and breaking out from the ordered pattern and rhythm of the bodily functions. One cell can disrupt the whole rhythm of any particular group of cells. For example, if you put particles of sand on a glass plate and arrange them in a certain pattern and order; then give one grain of sand a push and send it careering amongst the others, the whole pattern is disturbed. It breaks up. And when that particular grain comes to rest, the pattern is different."

"So you have to discover what makes that one cell go berserk?" I probed.

"I believe we know that" he answered. "That can be from two causes; an *outer* one, such as an actual force striking the cellular pattern (as with our example of the grain of sand) and this can result from a fall or a blow on the body. And an *inner* cause; pressure and tension built up in the mind and so reproduced in the body cells (which obey the mind up to a point), thus causing an obstruction. This muscle tension, or nerve tension can result in the collapse of some cells and the pushing out of place of others. Such tensions have many causes —worry, hate, fear, colour most of the lives on earth; frustration, anger, jealousy, inhibition and intense 'bottling up' of emotions (maybe from the highest motives but contrary to the freedom of the personality), all these are forces which concentrate themselves into extra tension on one organ and finally, on one cell . . . the 'rogue' which breaks away and starts a reproductive system of its own, really a production of a fungus. You know, Sister, if scientists and medical researchers studied the cause and production of fungi on plants, trees, roots, they would gain much insight into the rogue cell. . . ."

He was talking to me in language that I could comprehend. This excitement of his was infectious. I probed on.

68

He told me much that I could not quite understand, but back we came to the great Truth I am imbibing more and more though, as we know, its meaning was apparent in all our teachings on earth, if only we could follow them.

Light! Light! And yet more Light!

Light to educate and uplift the minds of the people, bringing calmness and peace in a sure reliance on life's Purpose and the wonder of Divine Creation. Light in their souls and in their minds to lift them above the *illusion* of earthlife's fears; Light in their minds to teach them how to 'tune in' any frustration of the life or personality to the great Reality of Divine Love. Naturally, this is the fact in Doctor X's revelations which appeals to me.

What man needs to discover, Doctor X went on, is some agent which would (using the example of the sand grain running amok), lure or force that single grain back into its correct place, or nullify it altogether and so restore the form and pattern. In the case of the first rogue cell at the outset of a cancerous growth medical science would do well to concentrate research to discover a powerful agent which would act as a restorer of this original life-pattern. Drugs, he says, should be tried and they will have partially favourable results. But it will be to the supreme benefits of *light* to which men must look for new techniques, new treatments, new restoratives; the light, he indicated, of the newly discovered, but only partially understood and employed Laser Ray.

Doctor X spoke of the use of a *pure Light Ray*, and I understood him to be referring to the Laser. In the future, he asserts, such a Ray will be used more extensively and can project its light on to these rogue cells. Later, he says, the Band will help to impress the minds of researchers with the realisation that, apart from its cutting power, this Ray, or rather a variation of it in modified form, can be used as a sort of catalyst to reform the cellular pattern which has gone awry.

Before this present century is out, Doctor X tells me, this method of employing Light will have become a great medical art and treatment to alleviate and arrest suffering.

At the same time man will be learning to govern himself, his mind, his emotions and his reactions to the purpose of creative thought.

69

Doctor X ended: "We are still on the palliative branch, but at least in the foreseeable future, medical men will be enabled to control the onslaught of cancer, as they have done such former scourges as diphtheria, typhoid and plague. Diagnosis of the early stages of cancer will be made by an adaptation of the present X-ray method and the rogue cells will be isolated. Then these will be treated by Light to nullify their mischievous distraction of the pattern form. As inoculation and vaccination have worked to stamp out former scourges of mankind, so the developed use of the Ray will finally reduce cancer as a killing disease to a minimum. . . . Research is being pursued actively and the 'seed-thoughts' of these revolutionary ideas are now being 'projected' into the minds of scientists and researchers in all nations . . . and which nation will get the 'break-through' first" he smiled, "is an interesting speculation for us."

The 'Daily Telegraph', 31st October 1968

CANCER CELLS DETECTED BY LASER LIGHT

A promising new way of detecting cancer cells, using laser light to illuminate them under a microscope, is being investigated at the International Research and Development Company's laboratories in Newcastle-upon-Tyne.

There is evidence that the malignant cells take on a brilliant red glow, while normal cells do not. This was first observed when scientists there started looking at malignant cells from the gut.

The technique was then tried on cervical smears from women, but with limited success.

The 'Daily Telegraph', 13th October 1966

NEUTRON USED AS CANCER TREATMENT

Scientists in Britain have started work on a new radiation device, using neutrons, which may be more effective than X-rays in the treatment of many forms of cancer.

Mr. James Wood, in charge of the project at the Ministry of Defence Services Electronics Research Laboratory, Baldock, Hertfordshire, said yesterday: "We cannot say definitely yet whether it will be a cure, but it looks like a fifty-fifty bet. It will take about three years to develop a neutron-generating tube with the high power output that is required. The end product is expected to be a machine compact enough to be installed in an ordinary radio-therapy treatment room. The neutron generation will be encased in fourteen inches of steel with a small aperture for the neutron beam. Mr Wood said that high-power output was needed so that treatment time could be cut down to a few minutes. This was the maximum time tolerable to a conscious patient.

Six weeks ago a tube of high-power was installed for the first clinical trials, but it still falls short of the required power output for routine patient treatment. It is being used for studies of cell damage and 'depth dose' characteristics.

Visitors to the laboratory's open days on Friday and next Monday and Tuesday will be able to see the neutron tube. The open days celebrate the laboratory's twentyfirst anniversary.

[Our Medical Consultant writes: The whole thing is entirely experimental. No one has cured a cancer with neutrons, even the cyclotron has not yet cured a cancer. Nothing has been proved.]

17th January

You must by now be realising the tremendous importance and reality associated with Light. If you recall, we worked on earth (as well as we could in the 'heavy' earth associations) trying to attain Light. But how difficult there to penetrate the inert forces which seemed to hold us. I wrote in my book *Frontiers of Revelation* of the experience I had of 'etheric light'; such experiences must be sought more positively, and with greater use of the intuitive powers, by those in the world who would wish to lift the slow vibration of the planet. . . . (More of this, perhaps, later.)

But to teach and learn by experience is the main reason for our communications to you. . . .

More and more positively I am stretching out into the Light. By thought and by will, the realisation of Light surrounding me, interpenetrating through every stratum of my being, has become my study, my concentration and my meditation at this stage.

When I am not 'on duty' with the souls in the Home who need care and help (and even then I make use of the Light!) I *will* myself into Light, asking that Light may be afforded me, that my soul and spirit may become as one infused Light; that I may live and move in the Light which is the Creative Will.

This is a wonderful, thrilling experience. When I caught but a glimpse of Light on earth, and it uplifted and changed me, and changed also the direction of my life, that impermanent glimpse was as *nothing* to the *immersion* of Light that is possible here. I appear to lie in my garden, yet in the power of this Light, my mind and spirit stretch out into a glorious extension. I become conscious (if only partially) of the world beyond world of thought, even beyond thought into Being. Psychiatrists would call these 'subjective experiences'. Yet what do any of us really know of the subjective *extensions* of the mind?

Here we are mind (stepped down to our individual potency, I grant), but still mind, untrammelled by the destructive and apparent reality of matter. . . . Therefore, by thought and will, we can travel far out beyond what constitutes our immediate circumstances, *if we wish.*

As I think I have stressed before, this stretching out into Light and Life can appear as a dream-extension. Yet, conversely, it is true and real to the dreamer! Perhaps it *is* Reality itself . . . at my present stage I cannot know.

Maybe I can illustrate by an experience, and the explanation of what happened (or appeared to happen, if you wish!) to me. I use the word 'appeared' guardedly, because I am still trying to synchronise an inner spiritual experience with the extension of the subjective mind of the psychiatrists, and the unconscious mind of the occultists, in earth terms.

But what I have learned and gained by my 'experience' is invaluable, thrilling and fills me with renewed hope and joy.

My experience happened during the last season of willing and praying myself into the Light. I was transported (how I do not know) to another Place, another Sphere, another 'mansion' in this world . . . maybe another planet, but of this I have no conclusive knowledge. Suffice it to say that suddenly and immediately I was conscious of being in a great 'atmosphere' of learning. I realised that I was in a university; yet it was much more than that, for there were Halls of Learning, and a pervading atmosphere of Thought which thrilled my soul and satisfied a deep yearning in me. The 'buildings' appeared Grecian in character, clean of line and symmetry. It was as though one imagined, or remembered perhaps in some deeply-buried soul-memory, how such buildings should look.

There were outer courts and beautiful vistas of gardens, where fountains of Light played. Here there were many souls, groups of students, sometimes surrounding One who appeared to be a Teacher, intent upon His discourse, or composed in deep meditation with Him; sometimes in clusters eagerly discussing together, and sometimes a student alone and apart in contemplation. These here were of all types and from all nations. I 'knew' that this man in his last incarnation on the earth plane had been dark-skinned. Here was a Chinese, an Indian, a Redskin. They were not different now, yet inwardly one was cognisant of the race to which they had latterly belonged. All had an air of concentrated clarity of thought and purpose, which clothed them like auras, brilliant and shimmering, yet varying in colour and in degree of intensity.

I was thrilled. I gazed around me and saw the inner Halls or maybe Temples. I noted that the doors of these stood wide open, yet none of the students in the outer courts seemed to proceed within. I wandered freely about amongst the groups, and through the avenues and groves. Here, here I told myself, is my University of the Spirit, and the memory of my longing for the materialisation of just such a university on earth filled me now with the new joy in this heavenly accomplishment.

I attached myself first to one group and then another. As I wandered, I thought I recognised faces that I had known, or figures familiar through their fame or their accomplishments on earth. Yet I could not be sure. I thought I saw your husband in one group in this court, intent, with others, on the discourse of a Teacher; too immersed in the subject, he only acknowledged me by a quick turn of the head, as though surprised to see me. I went on. I must find my place, I kept reiterating, in this great city of learning. I felt I was in some ecstatic dream, so uplifted and transported in my mind was I. *This is heaven* indeed. Always this has been my objective, like some half-forgotten vision of reality.

Now I *know*, I exulted, that such Universities of Discourse and

Study *exist. It is so.* And I too shall attend, when I discover the Teacher whose curriculum contains the knowledge I seek.

The thought came to me suddenly. What of the inner courts?

And I found myself with this speed of thought to which I am only slowly becoming acclimatised, ascending the steps towards one of the great doors which stood open. Here I felt, was revelation indeed!

But when I reached the top step a Light blinded me. The shock stopped any progress. I stood still, blank in mind and dazed, unable to push my way into this blinding flash. I was aware that the brilliancy of this Light was too much for my state.

Immediately, something seemed to be extinguished within me. My own light had become dimmed. I had the inexplicable experience of shrinking. Again I felt the strange, half-frightening sensation of dwindling . . . and dwindling. . . .

And I was back in my garden. This expansion of consciousness had been checked. I felt deflated! And defeated!

By what, I asked myself?

By my own egotism, my own inadequacy. I, who had not yet qualified for attendance in the outer courts, had dared to try to penetrate within. To say that my spirit was shaken is an understatement. . . . It has taken me periods of deep self-examination and earnest seeking for sufficient Light to see this experience in the clarity of unemotional understanding.

I was always too precipitate; always a seeker too eager to go on, and go forward, to break by force the frontiers of revelation. On earth (you remember?) I had envisaged a University of the Spirit; I had longed to be part of such a movement. I had worked with this glimpse of the vision in my mind.

The vision may have been right, but the approach to it savoured of egoism; the egoism of the limited human mind which has to be cleansed and stripped before the higher pattern of the spirit can manifest. I see now that the thought-pattern on earth is not geared sufficiently high above the material and the personal to hold such a possibility. I have had to learn too, that I am far from ready to participate as I had hoped . . . I am not yet entitled, it seems, to be enrolled in the outer courts of these Halls of Learning. . . . Perhaps, by the time of another incarnation? Who knows? One can only realise one's errors and go forward into greater understanding.

But now I am content. The vision is still with me, complete and satisfying; the hope of further teaching and progress. I must make myself ready by continued service, as well as by facing myself and learning of my defects, ready for that transition to a sphere for which my whole soul yearns.

Meanwhile, there is much to do, much to learn, so many new facets of this life with which to experiment, and finally to which to adjust; and always the Light is here, that Light of the Spirit which must be enhanced in me so that I can abide in It, and It in me. When this has, at last, been accomplished, even to some small measure, I know that I shall be allowed to proceed onwards towards my soul's desire; that is, to become a pupil in the outer courts, to mingle with those of great and exalted Minds, to listen to Truths propounded by Masters and Teachers of Wisdom, to imbibe such wisdom and to have my soul opened to the eternal Realities. Nothing stops one from doing what one wishes here . . . except one's own inadequacies!

17th January—Later

This is a world of thought indeed! So is the earth plane, you will say, from which I have just graduated. Only there, thought is slower in action because all vibration, and hence all results or effects, are slower, and one has a façade, a persona with which to mask thought.

Here one seems to be naked. There is no mask even for thought, one's inmost thought, and sometimes I shudder at the realisation that our fellows here can read us, as we read books illustrating character and thought and action on earth. Here, one's thoughts return to one like boomerangs, potent and immediate in their effects. As a thought, negative or positive, comes into mind, it is crystallised into immediate action. In the human mind, a negative thought can creep in and insinuate itself between all one's good intentions, lying, apparently dormant. Then it becomes a nucleus attracting to itself thoughts of similar content until it takes on a semblance of force through emotion; later the results, physical, material or spiritual, are manifested.

But in this new life, the *potency* of thought is stepped up into a frequency which permits of no side-stepping. The effects are

75

immediate. Here the *thought-pattern is determinate of one's welfare, one's progress, one's happiness and joy.* As one thinks, so one is ... in environment, appearance, and in company!

We have to learn to live in this new frequency; to guard the doors of one's mind; to anticipate the boomerang action of negative emotions. . . .

This is the way of life on these planes and every soul must assimilate the Way before proceeding onwards into planes of even higher frequencies. This is light and darkness as we know it; the day and night of the soul. . . .

18th January

There is an ex-policeman here; he has been in the Home for some little while, I mean *before* I arrived, and is soon being transferred to another station on this same plane for the reasons which I will explain.

He is a simple man. He was not educated, but had a great sense of duty and always fulfilled to the best of his ability . . . 'that station in life to which it had pleased God to call him', as we used to say. He was ailing for some time, I understand, before a sudden cessation of the heart function ended his life, and he came here. He was an honest man, who had never "bothered his head" (his words) about religion or philosophy; and he had supposed, as many still do, that death meant the end of all knowing. It has been a great wonder and astonishment to him to find life here so 'normal'. But he has responded well. It has taken time and much help on the part of the devoted workers here; but now that he is able to adjust to this new phase of living, he is anxious to help his family still on earth.

It appears that he had a son and a daughter, and was contented enough with his wife. The son is now in the force following in his father's footsteps; it is the girl who, he believes, needs his help. She was a pretty, wayward little thing, he told me, and at eighteen had an illegitimate child. He admitted, quite without repression, that he and his wife felt great shame at the time; nevertheless they accepted the child and brought it up as their own. After about two years the young mother deserted her family and her baby and went off to live with another man.

There were rows and recriminations. But she went her way and they had grown too fond of the child to send it away to a home. They saw less and less of their daughter; the baby grew into a healthy little girl, cared for tenderly by the grandparents.

Later, the daughter quarrelled with her protector, and went off with another man, then lived spasmodically with sailors at a southern port, and went steadily 'down the scale of respectability and morals' as he put it.

Naturally, the grandparents and the brother were upset, and longed and worked for the girl's return to a decent life. But every time they engineered a meeting it ended in scenes and accusations. Our policeman admitted, quite frankly, that his temper was not of the best, and that he invariably lost it during these meetings. So nothing constructive was ever managed. The grandparents were left with the child and the daughter went from 'bad to worse' (his turn of phrase is distinct, and very reminiscent of his upbringing), and she ended by openly becoming a prostitute or, as he phrases it, being 'on the streets'.

Poor man! Poor, sad angry father! Under the strain and worry his health deteriorated. He had to be relieved of his duties. Worry, fear, anger and a feeling of impotence with his daughter brought on the tension which caused the heart trouble. He collapsed.

He had told me of the 'inexplicable happenings of his dying'. He was rushed to hospital; the daughter was informed and, much to his surprise, she came to see him. She was actually at his bedside he believes, when he 'went out like a light' (his expression). But previous to that he was (as I was able to explain to him) unconscious to the earth world, yet he could hear what went on around him. As with all dying people, he could hear but he had no power either to think clearly or to speak. He was, however, perfectly aware of his daughter's grief. She wept bitterly and said that if only she could, she would come home again to live. He longed to say "Come home *now*" but his tongue would not obey him.

His wife said "Dad would want you to come home and be with us and your little one" but the girl only went on crying and saying that she was not fit to come home now.

After that he recollects that he must 'have had it' for he re-

77

members feeling an odd kind of rushing wind and then nothing more until he woke up here.

But you can realise how his thoughts and longings go out to his daughter. He no longer feels shame or anger, only a great desire to express his love for her and to help her redeem herself from the life she is leading. He has been told of the possibility of getting into touch with those on the earth plane, and *that* now, is our policeman's sole (and 'soul') desire. He wants nothing for himself; even the prospect of progressing onwards to work at anything he wishes does not appeal to him.

"I must find her" he keeps repeating. "If, as you say, there are ways for me to talk with her, then I must take them. I've got to say I'm sorry for my own harshness. I've got to show her that I love her; and I've got to tell her that I'm still alive ... living here, *compos* mentis and all ... and that she will live too!"

"But suppose she won't listen?"

"I'll keep on and on until she does!" he answered me, and there was a flash of the old stern personality, "I've got to prove this to her, for my sake as well as for hers, don't you see? Because all this is still so strange ... and wonderful! And because I've learned different now" he added, more quietly.

So at one of our Council meetings, we discussed his problem and it was decided to help our policeman on his way. There are Stations on this plane where communication with the earth plane is possible. (I always had an idea of this but now I know it is a fact.) In these Stations there are helpers and servers who have dedicated their knowledge and service to helping those who long to send messages to loved ones still on earth. The technique employed, I understand, is quite 'special' and very difficult at first to follow, even by those who desire to use it. But there *are* Stations, there are Directors for this work, there are administrators and (in a sense) technicians to run them.

You remember how, when I first knew you, I used to call you a 'celestial telephone'? Well I think of this sending out of messages from our side now as the 'earth telephone' or the 'telephone of the mortals' much to Father Joseph's amusement.

Privately, however, I think of it as a public telephone. At first I wanted very much to see how the work was carried on, even, perhaps, to try to send messages myself, until it became

78

clear to me that this would not only be a waste of effort but also a selfishness on my part, for I really have no need of this kind of help.

I have been fortunate enough always to have had an enquiring mind, and with this, as you know, I delved deeply into the subjects of communication and of Extra Sensory Perception. Telepathy, as you will confirm, we both studied and I practised it in my small way gaining some measure of success both with you and with others in unimportant experiences. But these methods of communication, via the astral plane, were (perhaps to my chagrin) never revealed to me. And I am convinced that there is no reason to pry now.

Thus, although I may visit our 'man in the force' in his new home and even watch him at the Station and try to help him, I shall keep to the methods which seem to suit the work I am trying to do . . . I mean, of course, our telepathic contact (and with others), in which my mind becomes 'tuned' to yours and can transmit and receive without need of other help . . . even that of a possibly bewildering technique.

For on this telepathic wave I can write with you these scraps of information on the all-controversial subject of Life after Death (though we are merely touching the fringe of all the wonders here and hereafter) with, I trust, satisfactory results . . . sufficient, anyway, to help those who may read.

This is part of my task now, and you who knew me so well were aware of my characteristic, that when I got my teeth into a subject, I would never let it go until sufficient knowledge had been extracted to satisfy me. . . . That trait serves me well here!

But now I am at liberty to tell you that this is not a solo performance on my part. Not by any means! There is a Band who help and guide me in the selection of incidents to be telepathed to you. In this, Father Joseph is most helpful, as he had contacted your mind previously; your husband also helped in opening the way and was instrumental in your listening to my mind in the first instance.

There are others in the Band, and I understand that we are merely instruments in this work. The veil between the worlds must be rent asunder (or dissolved as you suggest). People living on earth, the erudite, the cultured and clever minds, as

79

well as the devotional and religious minds, and the uneducated, the illiterate and the closed minds, must all be reached. All need this knowledge to remove fear which is one of the darkest and most powerful earth-emotions which has to be fought and conquered before peace and progress can come to the earth.

But still my great desire and trust is that I can continue working with you all in our Fellowship, and perhaps, widen the beliefs and perceptions of many souls by the Work which has been planned from our side in co-operation with your endeavours on earth.

23rd January

Your husband has been to the Home often and we have had long talks together. . . . I feel that I know and understand you much better now. . . . His information has cleared up much that was puzzling to me in your reactions to life and to people. I now understand you in a very different way from that which I thought I understood when we worked together on earth. . . . He has a great respect for your gift which, he says, he never appreciated when in the body. . . .

It seems to me now that we only understand properly and without emotional prejudices when we are separated from the life on earth. This seems such a pity and your husband agrees. How useless is remorse here . . . remorse for those things we did not do as well as for those we did—our actions mostly resulting from the fact that our minds, and therefore our reactions to circumstances, were clouded by partial judgment, and by preconceived (and often totally wrong) conclusions. We here, do regret these lacks very acutely, all the more so because scales have fallen from our eyes and we behold Truth (or perhaps I would be safer in saying 'a wider state of Truth' than could penetrate and neutralise the negative emotions of the body-mind).

I said that remorse here is useless . . . but that statement might have been too sweeping. To know all is to forgive all, so the more constructive thought one brings to bear on these regrets the better.

You should know well enough that 'get on with the job' was one of my precepts. Even with all eternity then before us it seems oddly wasteful to me to use up energy repining. Forgiveness, yes! Understanding of what was lacking and what went wrong . . . and confession to oneself of the sins of commission, and omission together with the acceptance of shame and failure.

Then a new beginning as the knowledge is turned into wisdom; an effort to right those wrongs, to help by love and concentrated direct thought to help where help is needed.

Some of the souls who come to our side and who have perpetrated much evil, take a great deal of advising and helping on this point. Remorse overwhelms them and often they choose to live in the gloom of regret. This is rightly termed 'gloom' (and I am not referring to the Place of Shadows) because, even here, by their sadness and remorse they are shutting themselves away from the very Light which could illumine their minds, dissolve their guilts and bring a constructive ray to bear on their problems. . . .

I have visited the 'lower regions' though, I assure you, with Conductors who were able to guide and protect us. Believe me it is a terrible region, or regions, of semi-gloom, of unwholesome 'sticky' emotions, of utter distortion of all that is beautiful. One's feelings are wrung by the pitiful sights; compassion flows out for those poor half-alive creatures in their self-darkness.

There are wonderful Helpers in these regions. These have to be advanced souls, strong in themselves and firm in the Light before they can choose to do such work. Whilst I was there on a visit, I saw the face of a Being of such beauty that I was arrested in my progress onwards and had to stop awhile just to be in the aura of this Great One. I learned afterwards that he had been almost a saint on earth. He was a great mystic, though an unlettered philosopher. Now he is the Leader of a Band of Helpers here and the Light of his countenance, though toned down for his patients to the potency they can stand, is glorious. My Conductor told me that this is his final training work and is a preparation for a high mission on which this great Soul will embark. I was not sure whether this presaged a return to earth conditions as a Great Teacher or Seer, or whether this is a prelude to undergoing further initiation into greater mysteries. I asked as many questions on the subject as could be answered, and was informed that he was indeed a Master of Wisdom and a most saintly soul, devoted to the Christ and one of a great band of potential World Redeemers. He has been in the Spheres for more than three centuries, as time is reckoned on earth, and has 'passed through' many of the Higher Planes, being a Member of a Brotherhood of Light. His selfless service here is an unspoken lesson. The Sisters reverence Him. Some of them have joined his Band of Helpers and have worked under His Direction, returning to the Home for rest and recuperation after the arduous duties. I know that Father Joseph often visits here and works in the Band.

I 'returned' to my cottage and my golden garden with a feeling of relief, together with a great joy and appreciation of the Light here. I thought a lot about those words . . . 'They that sit in darkness and the shadow of death' and a new meaning and connotation was added to our old scriptural one. That place was *shadow* indeed. The *shadow of death*, but not so definitely the death of the body as the death of the *mind*, for there the mind is *inert* in the *density* caused by the wrong use of a God-given faculty, man's mind and freewill. This density causes the soul to be starved to such a deficiency as to render it 'cut-off' and its Light shut away. Surely that is death . . . or rather the *shadow of death*?

This, to me, is far more frightening in its implications than the explanation we, on earth, accept for that phrase. Death of the body is merely a change. The 'shadow' of death is a gruesome *fact*, but thank God, a fact that will never be experienced by those who try to live the good life and to open their minds to Truth.

And to this phrase 'the Good Life' I do not attach any sloppy interpretation. The Good Life as those here see it, is not a sentimental vague dream of goodness, neither is it the ego-swelling do-gooding and praying publicly which Jesus condemned in the Pharisees. As I am learning here the following of the true Inner Light, the obedience to the guiding of that Light and the consequent work and action prescribed by the wisdom of that Light, these constitute the Good Life, the full life, the life more abundant of the scriptures of all religions.

'A soul-infused personality', remember, was a phrase I used very much on earth, and probably with a false interpretation of its true meaning? Now that I have seen this great Master-Soul in His humble capacity and service, the realisation of what

Soul is has been impressed upon me, never, I trust, to be forgotten.

Soul is Light infused . . . or infused Light.

The shutting away of the soul is darkness.

As the sun is the carrier of light-beams to the earth, so is the Son, the Second Manifestation of the Divine Energy of Creative Mind, the transmitter of Light beams to the soul. 'They that sit in darkness' reject the beams from the Son and so are in death, the shadow of death.

May Light descend on earth.

Then the terrible illusions of these shadow places will be dispelled forever.

4th February

You ask about precognition and whether it is a fact that the future is foreseeable. As far as my experience goes, and as far as this new extension of my consciousness reveals facts about earth-life time, I am becoming increasingly aware of a Pattern and a Plan. The Blueprint of one's efforts, one's successes and failures on all the planes; physical, material, emotional, mental and spiritual does indicate that a definite line of advance is voluntarily accepted by the soul *before incarnation*.

No doubt when I am more proficient in the study of individual lives and their results, together with the life courses of nations and their results, good or apparently not good, which have been set in motion through the Law of Cause and Effect, I shall be better able to appreciate how the Divine Pattern of individual growth and group growth is linking up from life to life and from age to age. It is only logical to assume that we take up, as it were, where we left off in a previous trial of strength and weakness. This presupposes a chain of lives, of experiences, of reincarnation in its little understood form. But I am more than convinced, as I observe stories of effort and success and failure, that the soul needs to 'project' some part of Itself back into the denser environment of earth in repeated attempts to master the trials and stresses of those vibrations. But which part of Itself, and whether it is always the same part, is still a mystery, and must remain so until we have advanced much in wisdom and insight.

After talking with savants I have been privileged to meet here there seems no reason for me to change my earthly acceptance of the fact of repeated lives, and therefore of a possibility of pre-viewing the presentable future, even when in a material body. When a soul (or that portion of a soul which seeks enlargement of experience) reincarnates, it is at a certain stage in its Divine Blueprint. It will seek a trial of strength in some experiences, a leading role in human affairs in others, an emotional compensation in personal relationships and so forth. Therefore, up to a point, it fixes its own 'coming events' because they will afford it the necessary experience it has come to gather, and these will be commensurate with the overall Pattern associated with its progress. It must react, in a way, consistent with its stage of development and thus on its path will be mapped highlights of attainment, humble or elevated in its particular sphere of influence, together with despondencies and failures which, to the Inner Eye, *can be foreseen*.

As it is possible here to review the incidents in one's life on earth with the causes which led up to these incidents, and the effects which they brought, together with the lessons they teach, so it is feasible to assume that the process can work forward as well as backward. In other words, as there is no such thing as time, the beginning, ending and the actual event are all one. Therefore, in a soul which has retained this 'negation of time' in its consciousness on earth, the possible future can be discerned. That there are mistakes made and unfounded sweeping assertions promulgated still does not negate the truth of this fact. The human mind can be deflected by human emotions, egotism, self-centredness and pride and such emotions cloud the issue of truth. But the fact remains that the possibility is there, the future springs out of the past. That certain seers have always been able to predict does not imply preordained patterns of existence in the rigid sense. It does illustrate the reality of timelessness . . . that each moment holds in itself, all of the past and of the future.

In new experiments into space exploration, the fact of 'weightlessness' has proved itself. In the 'foreseeable future' (so I am informed by those who know more of the Pattern and the Plan) souls in incarnation on earth will be enabled to prove the *fact of timelessness*, and this by scientific process and experiment (possibly in that very space the scientists have set out to explore). It will be as exciting a discovery as this last advance in weightlessness and non-gravitational pull.

Through the truth inherent in this 'new' knowledge, mankind will make an immense leap forward into Light. For as knowledge is increased a thousandfold, so is responsibility in following the Pattern increased a millionfold.

This is a great point of realisation for all incarnate, as well as discarnate souls. I trust we all will learn.

7th February

Yes. I teach and I am being taught. I am able to give service to others who, through unfortunate circumstances of birth or environment, or owing to prejudice which is often a component of ignorance, have not learnt even the rudiments of *living*.

Many who arrive here are either completely overwhelmed by the fact of a further existence, or disillusioned because in their narrow creeds, they have envisaged a heaven of utter delight which, to such crude imaginations, included the joyful inference that from henceforth no efforts would ever be needed by them. In fact, a blessed state of negativity, of passive acceptance, of paradise, a kind of super-Welfare State where they would dream away Eternity.

But this is certainly no super-Welfare State.

It is, indeed, a state of welfare, which has a different meaning altogether, and super, yes, if by that adjective we describe an existence where beauty is manifest, where negative or unkind thoughts are prohibitive because such thoughts are visible and audible, where help and love are always at hand to help the traveller, and where every circumstance points to a greater Life, a wider understanding and the glorious certainty of progress after effort and exertion.

This is an existence in another dimension of thought; disease, poverty, cruelty, suffering as it is known on earth could not possibly exist here, because the Light of the Spirit opens our vision and we seek the Way to Higher Worlds of even more glorious beauty.

Yes, I am teaching here. I am also learning compassion, for

the limited consciousness which belongs to those who did not have the opportunities afforded to me of studying the mysteries of life.

Our work is to be on hand when those newly arrived entities awake to awareness. Sometimes their friends and loved ones already in these realms have been 'alerted'. Then we wait in the background until the greetings are over. In other cases ours are the first 'countenances' they see; ours are the words of comfort, assurance and welcome.

Our 'patients' stay with us until they have adjusted to this new life and are ready to join their dear ones or their special Groups. This may be only a short passing phase or a longer 'period' according to their state of development. According to the reactions after the first shock of individual examinations of Blueprints of their earth lives, so is our method of helping them. With understanding, extreme gentleness and certainly no hint of censure, the Sisters explain the Rest Home and its purpose. The newcomers are then introduced to the idea of an expanding progress and are encouraged to right the wrongs they have done in their earth lives by concentrated thoughts of forgiveness and compassion.

I suppose you could call this a hospital, a home of rest upon the Way and a 'kindergarten' teaching-centre. All these terms would be correct. The weary souls, the frightened souls, the ignorant and 'fallen' souls, together with those who have been 'rescued' from the 'Land of Shadows' require understanding and explanation of their sore states, and there are some to whom Survival has to be explained, even demonstrated. Many will not accept the fact of death, or prefer to consider that they still dream. You see how wide is our work and how, by teaching, we ourselves learn. By demonstrations of the results of other lives, I myself have learned much and I am still learning.

Many of the Sisters of my former community on earth have now passed on to Higher Spheres, but dear Mother Florence remains from choice, although she too visits other planes for refreshment and, I imagine, for reward. Other Sisters from similar communities join us and work with us and of these Sister Ursuline has become a companion to me. We have much in common and I admire her many gifts and her clear, logical mind. She will be going on to work at another 'Receiving Station', for ours, I understand, is only one of many such Homes for Healing.

But I am also taught, not so much by lectures or books, though I still read much, as by discussion and by example. More of this later.

9th February

This is indeed a world of thought. *You* live, of course, also in a thought world, only with you, thought has been crystallised very deeply into matter and much of the illusion of that existence has become 'solidified' in the earth mind. Mind has often closed away reality from itself. Here we are what we appear.

In the body one can mask one's true self, as well as one's Self, and appear very different from reality. Here the persona, or mask, has been removed and our very thoughts are open to all. Think what that would mean on earth! This new interest in many of the world's scientists in Extra Sensory Perception, especially in the fact of *Telepathy*, will result in a wearing away of this persona mask, for through it, disloyalty, insincerity, lying, will be disclosed. In future developments in this and the next century, thoughts will indeed become things, as they are in essence and able to be 'read'. Man will learn that truth in all things is essential. As we learn it here.

Anger, irritation, depression can actually be *seen* in the appearance and 'field' surrounding an entity. They can actually be felt and sometimes 'heard' as a low warning, drumming, rather like a wasp's buzzing. I have experienced this in others, and alas, other dear souls have avoided me for the same reason at times.

Thoughts are truly things. That is why, when an entity comes over to this plane he, or she, automatically graduates to the rightful plane. That is Law. It also explains why some folk are so surprised and dismayed at their surroundings. For instance, one who has lived an ordinary good life shall we say, doing the right things, attending to his outward religious observances, but all the time concealing within himself black thoughts of envy, malice, uncharitableness, will find himself in the company of such as he is, and sometimes of those worse than he is. Dismay

87

will fill his soul until he realises that this great Law is just, and until he makes efforts to adjust his thinking to Love, Charity, Truth and to try to redress the wrongs he has worked on others. In these efforts there is always help at hand, always more advanced souls ready to comfort, to listen and to teach him. There are souls too, ready to guide him to higher realms and to happier company.

Progress is as open here, more so indeed, and as satisfying in reward as any success on the earth plane. One has only to have a glimpse of the Planes of Mind, where emotions have been conquered and transmuted into aspiration, to realise the wonder of Creation and the Love of God for His creatures. One has only to see the dark misery of the self-imprisonment of souls in the shadow-worlds to understand the justice and the balance of the Life Force.

When telepathy and mind-communication become more widespread in the world, then will Light be raised up in man and he will realise his oneness with all. Then will the meaning of Peace on Earth, Goodwill to Men, become apparent. Then will the veil of darkness, the belief in matter, begin to dissipate and the thought force of man be lifted into constructive manifestation. Then will man graduate from the shadows towards the Light, from misery to joy, from ignorance to knowledge, from illusion to reality. And then will the world know peace.

Let Light descend on earth.

17th February

Let me tell you about Jeannie. Jeannie lived to be nearly twelve years old on earth. She was a pretty, fairy-like child, daintily made. Her whole ambition was to become a dancer and she began to train when she was very young, showing, I believe, a fair talent. Unfortunately at the age of eight she contracted polio, a very severe case, and was, for some months, kept in an iron lung.

She recovered but one leg was shrunken; it continued to shrink the muscles appearing to be withering away. The poor child was in and out of hospitals for months. She underwent several operations; she wore a brace on her leg, but the muscles continued to shrink until one leg was noticeably shorter than the other. She was often in much pain but the greatest sadness to this child was in the loss of her dancing life.

She couldn't bear to think that she would never dance again, never be in the corps de ballet, never have the happiness of performing what she loved to do. In the hope of having the leg restored to normal state she stoically underwent the several tortures of stretching tackles, iron clamps and further operations.

In the end, and at the age of eleven years, she knew that she would never be as other girls, she would never hop, or jump, or run again. The agony to her mind and emotions of this realisation and the constant bouts of illness weakened her constitution. At twelve years old, after a chill, she died of pneumonia.

When Jeannie 'woke up' here in our Home Mother Florence and I were at her bedside. The child looked about her, trying to focus her sight on these new surroundings. At last she saw us. She stared hard, then her little face crumpled and she burst into tears.

"It's the Sister. I'm back in the hospital again" she wept. "Please, please don't make me have any more operations. . . ."

Mother Florence patted her hand.

"You are only in our Home for a rest" she said. "You're going to be quite well again, Jeannie . . . quite, quite", she emphasised the word 'well'.

The child looked at Mother Florence.

"Are you the matron?" she asked.

Mother nodded. "If you like to call me that. But this is not a hospital, only a rest home, and you are getting well very quickly."

Jeannie turned her head away.

"No," she said, "I'll never be well. I've got a shrunken leg."

"Not now, Jeannie," I volunteered, "Not any more. Your leg is well, quite well and strong."

The child shook her head.

"Look at it yourself" Mother urged. "It's just as long as the other one. Take a look and see."

"But I know it isn't" Jeannie couldn't be persuaded. "I know you're only saying that. . . . Where's my Mummy?"

"You can go and see her presently" Mother suggested "when you've learned to run again."

"Run?" Jeannie's attention was caught.

"Yes. Run." I bent over her "We're going to teach you to run and play and dance here, Jeannie."

Her eyes brightened.

"Dance?"

"Yes dance." I took hold of her legs, gently raising them. "Look, Jeannie, they're both the same length, see?"

Jeannie stared. She looked from one to the other of us. Slowly she sat up. She ran her hands up and down her calves, over the ankles, fingering the bones of the feet carefully and then back to the knees. She did this over and over as if she couldn't believe that which she could feel and see. She was silent, puzzled. It evidently never occurred to her to try to stand up. Habit was still too strong. She just sat there holding her legs and gazing down at her feet. Presently she looked up at us.

"Is it a miracle?" she asked in an awed voice.

"You could call it a miracle" Mother answered and the smile that illumined her face was truly beautiful.

Jeannie was silent, considering this.

"Are you the Virgin Mary?" she asked at last.

"No I'm not the Virgin Mary, dear."

"You look like Her", and I too thought how lovely was the face beneath the plain veil, "and *She* does miracles."

Mother smiled. "Supposing you get up and stand" she suggested.

"Without my crutches?"

"Yes. Try."

"Will it hurt?"

"No. You won't have any pain. You'll never have that old pain again, Jeannie."

"You promise? I really won't?"

Suddenly Jeannie caught my hand and clung to it.

"I promise" we both said. She nodded. It was plain that she was not sure that she could trust us.

"Won't you try to stand??" asked Mother again. She did not make an answer, but she allowed me to lift her legs and set them down. We held her little body and slowly we raised her to her feet. She staggered and swayed, terrified to put any faith in the once-crippled leg. After waiting, she put down her foot, but still clutched at our support. Slowly her expression changed. Surprise, incredulity, belief, joy, spread over her face. She let go of us. She stood erect, balancing on both feet. She even moved forward a few paces.

"It's true. It's true. It *is* a miracle!"

Suddenly, overcome with this great and joyful awakening, she sank back on to the bed and she sobbed for pure happiness. "I shall walk again," she cried. "I'm well. I'm like other girls!" Her eyes clouded, she looked piteously at me. "Unless I'm dreaming. . . ."

"You are *well*, Jeannie," I insisted, "and it isn't a dream. It's true."

She smiled. It was obvious that this had all been a great strain for her. She was becoming weary. She would need rest. One's first return to consciousness after one's transition is often overwhelming and this was no exception.

"Then if this is true . . . we must say a prayer . . . a thanks . . . a Hail Mary."

Mother Florence bent over the child.

"Would you like us all to thank God with you?" she asked gently. The girl nodded. She closed her eyes. Together we spoke softly the Prayer of Thanksgiving. As we prayed, Jeannie slipped back into the passive state of the newly-awakened into this consciousness. So we let her rest.

Jeannie was my constant companion. We went for long walks together; we vied with each other in finding the most beautiful flowers; we ran hand in hand down the long slopes of the hills and it was a joy to watch the child. She danced and whirled and twirled about as lightly as a butterfly. She ran from flowers to flowers; she skipped and sang and laughed for pure joy.

I have discovered that she has a well-developed mind. Perhaps the years of sickness, the enforced rests, and the consequent periods of reading and thinking have developed a deeper stratum of thought than was usual in children of her age. She has a philosophical bent and a wisdom that is surprising in one so young.

Did I say young? Her soul is not young. She is, I should judge, an advanced soul. She seems to 'know' so much without even having been told. I recall her manner of accepting death, naturally and solemnly. Nobody had actually said anything of this transition. She was allowed to rest until ready to move. Then she walked about the grounds of this beautiful home to her heart's content. She was carefully shielded, of course, from our 'sick' patients.

I came upon her in my garden.

"Do you want to see my flowers?" I asked. She shook her head.

"I've come to see you, Sister". There was a pause. Her eyes regarded me with direct candour. "I've just realised something."

I waited.

"I've realised that I'm not dreaming" she said quietly. "I'm dead." Her gaze held mine. "We're all dead. That's true, isn't it?"

"Yes. It's true, Jeannie" I answered her "but you see we're really more alive than ever. You've only got rid of your sick old body and found a new one. . . ."

She accepted this.

"I suppose this is . . . a sort of Heaven."

"It's the *beginning* of Heaven, Jeannie."

"You mean we're only *starting*? . . . We're not *there* yet?"

"Not in the Heaven you mean, Jeannie. But we're on our way there."

She digested this. "But it's so beautiful here. Everyone's so kind and . . . and . . . angelic."

"We're certainly not angels." I retorted and we both laughed at that. She was quiet suddenly.

"Then where's God?" she demanded.

"Much too far away for us even to see Him. We're not ready for His Glory yet. But we're all going forwards, on towards His Heaven. . . ."

"You mean, His Heaven could be better than this?"

"Oh, much, much better! Far more beautiful and full of Light, and angels, Angels of Light. . . ."

She smiled at me. We were both silent whilst she thought this out.

"I see" she agreed. Her face lit up. "I like that . . . Angels of Light. . . ."

At another outing she said, quite suddenly. "I hope Mummy

won't miss me terribly. I don't think she will, you see I was always ill and then there are the others. Mummy was always so busy."

"You had brothers and sisters?"

"Yes. They weren't like me. They were well." She considered gravely for a moment. "I'd like to talk to Mummy though. Can I?"

"We can try, Jeannie. But it isn't easy to reach your mother. You see those who can 'hear' us on earth must have developed an 'inner telephone'."

"I don't think Mummy had an 'inner telephone'. We had a telephone, of course, an ordinary one, and I liked talking into it."

For awhile we both watched a shaft of Light that seemed to glow beyond where we sat. "I'd like to *see* Mummy again . . . and see what she's doing. Can I?"

"We can try" I answered, recalling my own experiences at the Memorial Services. "You tell me what your mother is like and your house and your brothers and sisters, and I'll see if we can make a picture. . . ."

"And we can 'go down' through that picture, is that it?"

She had caught on quickly to this new 'game'.

"Yes, that's it."

We tried. She described her mother, her father, her family, her home on earth. I did my best to concentrate and to 'project' us into the picture.

We were silent for so long that I wondered if indeed Jeannie had 'found' her people. She lay on the grass beside me, her face very rapt and expectant. At last she sighed.

"I can't *see* Mummy . . . but I feel that I'm near her . . . I think she *knows*. I'm trying to tell her that my legs are both the same length and that I can walk and run now. Oh, I *want* her to know that, Sister. Do you think she does?"

"I'm sure she has an inner feeling about it, Jeannie."

"Mummy isn't unhappy about me . . . not really" the child went on. "I *feel* that she knows I'm in Heaven and she's glad about that. I am really aren't I?"

What could I answer!

"Darling, you are very near Heaven." I said. I was thankful that this explanation had been put into my consciousness.

93

"I suppose this is Life Everlasting?" she persisted. I had to think out my reply.

"We have always been in Life Everlasting, Jeannie, even when we were on earth. Our souls, our true Selves, always have lived from experience to experience. This is only another *part* of experience."

She took this very seriously. "And Heaven will be another experience?"

"There will be many experiences I believe, my dear, even before we reach Heaven."

"You mean where God is?"

I nodded. "Yes, that must be a most glorious Sphere."

Presently she said: "I never went to Church or Sunday School much. I couldn't of course, and my parents weren't very religious. But the nuns in the hospitals used to talk to me. They told me stories about Jesus and the Saints. You believe in the Saints, don't you, Sister?"

"Of course. They are the Wise Ones, the Great Ones, and they have communion with the Angelic Host."

"Do you think I shall ever see Them?"

I was moved to say a blessing on this sweet, innocent soul. "Yes. You'll see Them, Jeannie."

"And the Angelic Host . . . the Angels of Light?"

I nodded. "And the Angelic Host." I agreed. (Very likely before I shall, I thought to myself.)

She said quietly. "I hope I do. You see, in hospital, I used to ask little Sister Thérèse to make my leg grow to the same length as the other one. I'm sure she heard me. . . . Perhaps, sometime, I'll see her . . . really see her. . . ."

"Perhaps." I said.

I clearly remember her visit to my garden not long before she left us. Then she burst out "Mother Florence says when I'm ready I'll go to the Halls of Beauty . . . that's in another part of Heaven. . . . She says I'll see the greatest dancers in all the world there, Greek dancers, Indian dancers, Pavlova and Nijinski, and oh, heaps of others! She says I'll learn to dance, really learn I mean and that I'll be able to join with these others in the great Dance Festivals. Do you believe that, Sister?"

"Mother Florence knows much more about the Spheres than I do." I agreed. She pirouetted up and down on her toes before my flower bed.

"Oh, it will be lovely! I'll work so hard and I'll be good. I do mean to be ready soon. Of course, I'll miss you and Sister Hilda and Mother Florence and everybody, but I want to go so much. I must go soon. You see," she stopped dancing, quietened and stood still before me, "You see, I've got to be perfect at dancing before . . ." she broke off.

"Before what, dear?"

She swung herself round so that I couldn't look at her face.

"Before I go back to the earth again . . . really to be a dancer."

For a while I was silenced, overwhelmed by the wisdom of this child.

"Who told you that you would return to earth?" I asked at length. She still averted her face.

"It was the Angel" she told me. "He came when I was resting. And *He* told me. . . ." She returned and regarded me solemnly. "You know, I think He was *my* Angel. I seemed to have known Him before."

What was there to answer to this? Out of the mouth of this babe, I, who had vowed myself to the religious life, was being given the answers. I felt very humble indeed. . . .

Jeannie recovered very quickly from the strangeness of her transition. She adjusted to this new life with all the flexibility of a child's unspoiled nature. To her everything was a revelation. I shall ever think of her as a happy, dancing soul. One of the Band of Beauty in God's Plan.

She left us very quietly. One moment she was there, laughing, dancing, chattering amongst us all. Then we became aware of a Being standing beyond the shade of the trees; a Man of Light, tall, graceful with the beautiful limbs of a dancer. He stood in the Light and he held out his hand.

"Come, Jeannie" he said. She ran to him immediately. Then she turned. Her little face was transfigured with joy.

"It's the Messenger" she cried. "Isn't it wonderful! Wonderful."

She waved to us all. "Thank you for what you have done for me. Thank you for helping me get well. Now I shall really dance. You will come to the beautiful Place to see me some-time won't you? Won't you?" She put her hand with perfect trust into the hand of the Messenger. "Goodbye."

"Farewell for a space" we called back.

Together the two walked down the long sunlit slopes, and the Light of the Messenger seemed even brighter than the Light shimmering over our gardens. Then they were gone . . . and I, for one, felt that we had given back a ray of sunshine to the Great Creative Sun.

I miss Jeannie, of course. That child, by the fine quality of her nature, had taught me much. Beauty as such, in the creative arts of dancing and movement, had been absent from my earth life altogether. Now I realised how much I had missed. For Beauty is surely an attribute of God . . . and the art of the dance is a manifestation of that attribute.

I hope that I shall see Jeannie in her Hall of Beauty Festivals sometime. It will be a great and moving moment.

17th February—continued

When I was in the Community I spent some periods on missionary work in the hinterlands of South Africa. I remember telling you about my journeys out over the rough roads, of our old jogging mule and the funny little hut in which I was 'housed' for my visits.

Well I have, with Mother Florence's permission, been al-lowed to accompany her and some of the Sisters on their missionary work into the Shadow Lands. It is a salutory ex-perience. I am specially being instructed to recount the sad adventure to you, that it might be included in the book. For it might be of use in clarifying the illusory ideas on the states of Heaven and Hell which have been fostered through the centu-ries.

There are Heavens . . . I myself can vouch for the little heaven of beauty, tranquillity and loving service which it has been my happy lot to contract here. But there are Spheres of unimaginable joy and beauty beyond . . . building up and ex-tending out of every state of development . . . right on, I be-lieve, to the Spiritual Worlds of Divine Thought, far beyond any conception you and I can have of them. Such is the progress of the soul towards these Spheres of Perfection and it is assuring to realise that we have all Eternity in which to journey onwards and 'upwards'.

But there are also Hells though certainly differing from the physical hells and everlasting fiery torments of man's warped imagination. There are hells of the spirit and the mind, confining states of misery; dark, depressing and as real as the tortured consciousness of the dweller therein makes them. Yet these hells are not eternal. The man (or woman) in these mental torments need stay there no longer than his desires keep him. He is free to resist the hatreds, cruelties, lusts of his lower nature which he has retained from his earth life and which are keeping him in dark dungeons amid like-minded inhabitants. He can always choose to follow the Light of Love, Forgiveness and Harmony and always there are souls ready to help, to guide, to comfort and to assist.

No soul is ever left comfortless unless he wishes it.

That sounds like a paradox, but then much that we learn here is very different from the teachings of man, even good men who are limited in their ideas. Existence on earth is a state of living in a thought world, illusory, and much restricted and enclosed by the glamorous web of matter. Beyond physical death the thought world is more apparent and certainly far more potent in its effects. Cause and Effect is still the Law on this plane of astral matter, as it is on earth. I understand that only as the soul proceeds onward in its progress into Higher Realms can this Law be superseded, and then other and higher Laws must be obeyed. But to my mission.

Mother Florence, two other Sisters and I, made our journey into what you would call, the Underworld. Here we prefer the description Shadow Land, for this is indeed a Land of Shadows. The journey to this place is difficult and wearying for we have, by concentrated thought power, to 'slow down' our vibrations so that our 'bodies' will be enabled to endure the physical conditions pertaining therein. The Sisters never go without the special Messengers who guide them there and conduct them to the various stations on the way.

The Shadow Land is a very real place indeed; a gloomy murk covers it to which one has to become accustomed; squalid dwellings inhabited by unhappy, tormented beings who jeer

97

and mock and pursue their warped existences. Sometimes these poor souls live in hatred and rebellion, sometimes in apathy and sometimes with a fierce denial that there is any other state of existence possible.

But I must tell you of the painter whom I met; an artist who lives in a dreary little 'room' in a dark and crooked street in Shadow Land, yet who still cherished in his soul some remembrances of beauty.

He was, on earth, a Frenchman, a painter of promise, who dissipated the gift which God had entrusted him. He spent his life in riotous laziness, indulging in drink and drugs, until he was reduced to the gutter. Eventually he was mixed up in a night brawl, during which he killed a fellow artist, and himself received a knife wound from which he later died.

I must have become separated from the others of our little band for I found myself alone in this narrow street with its uneven cobbles and narrow pavements between the dwellings. Seated before an easel at the curb edge was the painter. He was splashing greasy oil colours on to his canvas. He was short and squat, with a mass of dark hair which bunched untidily about his face and he appeared to be wearing a dirty grey overall.

As I stopped to view his work he looked up and scowled at me. The painting, I observed, was dull and uninspired. It consisted of great shapeless masses which I concluded were meant to represent his fellow beings. They looked dreary enough in all conscience, and all in unrelieved sombre hues.

When he took no notice of me I asked:

"Is this your studio? May I be allowed to see your other canvases?"

He scowled again, but he jerked his head towards the open door nearby in a gesture which I took to be of assent. I went into the cluttered room. It was a dark little hovel of a place with only one window and that too dirty to admit anything but a faint twilight. The walls were stacked with canvases. At first I was so nauseated by the strong penetrating smell of the room that I was unable to do anything. When, however, I became used to the odours I was able to give my attention to the paintings.

I began to examine them closely. They were all the same;

all dark, all hideous, all primitive and almost evil in their sardonically clever interpretation of character and all exceedingly ugly. But there was one strange feature common to all of them. A door.

Painted into the background of each picture there was always a door, dark brown in colour, and always closed. The door was always of the same pattern, and of the same mahogany tone. But always there was a faint line of white outlining it, this effect had been attained by leaving a wisp of white canvas exposed.

I studied the paintings with great care and was immediately interested from a psychological point of view, for the door was always represented, its dark panels closing away a suggestion of light. . . . After a little I became aware that the painter was standing at my elbow.

"Well," he growled and if he spoke in his native tongue I understood perfectly in mine, "so you don't like them."

"They're too gloomy" I said.

He waved his arms wildly. "Too gloomy? I defy anyone to do any other in this stinking hole."

"Why do you stay here then?"

He glared. "Oh, drop dead! Why do I stay? Do you think I would if I knew a way out?"

I turned as if to leave. "There is a way out" I remarked, casually. He kicked viciously at a canvas.

"Same old missionary stuff. I've heard it all before. A lot of blasted prejudiced saviours. And you're all living in illusion, same as me."

The strange answer indicated a mind not wholly obliterated.

"I'm neither blasted nor prejudiced." I kept my voice as cool as thought could make it. "That seems to be a description of yourself." He was most affronted.

"What the hell . . ."

"*You* are blasted, living in this place" I pointed out, "I should imagine anyone would be, and you are prejudiced because you've closed your mind to anything else."

"Anything else?" he roared. Suddenly, with a change of tone, as he swung round to face me. "And is there anything else?"

"Yes" I said confidently "There is."

"Tell me" he jeered.

This was not going to be easy.

99

"There are places here" I felt my way carefully into what I wanted to impress on him "where painters like yourself live and paint the natural beauties of the countryside."

"Ah!" his temper had modified a little. "So it is the old, old story. I've been told it all before you know."

I nodded. "Nevertheless, you still hold to your prejudices? You won't believe, even if you keep on being told?"

"How can I?" He glared about him, snatched up a canvas, crumpled it and threw it into a corner. "I ask you how can I? I've been in Hell too long. . . ."

"Yes—too long!" I dared to interrupt.

"Perhaps I've become accustomed to it . . . it's been a hell of a long time. They brought me here from the hospital. Though I haven't yet worked out what happened to me. I was unconscious, I think . . . and then I found myself here. Nobody seems to know why. And anyway I wouldn't ask the old sots— they don't know *anything* here. Nor care to find out . . . I keep myself to myself. . . ." He gave me a wicked grin. "I'm not the type, lady, for confessions and that sort of thing. . . ."

"Then what are you doing but confessing your prejudices and fears to me?"

"Bah!"

"You're making your own hell, you know."

He swept out his arm in an eloquent gesture. "*I* never made this."

"Not actually, only by your thoughts you have . . . just as the others have done."

"The others here? Blasted crows! Haven't an idea in their heads. They don't even know the differences between light and shade. . . ."

"And do you?" I pointed deliberately to the masses of dingy colour in his picture.

His temper rose at once.

"Yes, I do!" he roared. He stalked across the room, back to his easel, glared at the half-finished canvas on it. "Damn your eyes. I could paint once. I *did* paint I tell you, really paint. . . ."

"But not now?"

Suddenly he was quiet, anger spent. "Could *you* paint here?" he whispered. I glanced at the mediocre dwellings in the street, the contorted faces of the individuals who passed by outside, the dirt, the squalor.

"I wouldn't try."

"Ah!"

"Why don't you try to find other places?" I suggested, as he did not speak.

"Other places?"

"Where it is light and beautiful."

He watched my face as he pondered this.

"You *know* such places?"

"I know them."

He shrugged. "Me? How could I get to them? I have nothing, no money, no pass, no tickets. How could I ever get to such places?"

I was about to reply when I become conscious of Mother Florence standing beside us. I had been so absorbed that I had forgotten the others with whom I had made the journey to these hells of thought.

"By looking for them" Mother Florence interposed very gently. "By *asking* to be taken to the places of Light."

He stared at her. Disbelief, distrust stood out around him like a dark cloud.

"You're *sure* there are such places?" he demanded but now there was a harsh expectancy in his manner.

"Oh, yes!" we both answered him and I hoped that I did not sound too pressing. "We know them."

"But I have no ticket of admission."

"You have" Mother Florence reminded him in her soft way. "You have *thought*."

"Thought? Well?"

"Think about Light" she said. "Paint Light into your canvases."

He was immediately exasperated by our apparent stupidity. "How can I paint Light?" he shouted "when I haven't got the colours . . . the light colours?"

"You can always get them. One of the Helpers will give you the light colours" Mother answered calmly. "Wait, I will call one now."

Immediately a young man wearing a brown cassock stood beside us.

"Our artist friend" Mother indicated the painter "needs cleaner colours. He wishes to paint Light into his pictures. . . ."

The Brother's smile was welcoming.

"Splendid. Come, my friend, I will get you new tubes of colours. We will see that you can paint Light. Come. . . ."

Hunching his shoulders in a gesture of astonishment at these strange happenings, the painter turned and followed the robed figure. We watched them walk together up towards a hill where the gloom was threaded with a spear of brightness. Mother Florence's smile was quite beautiful.

"He's on his way, Sister" she said, then, with the characteristic little shake of her head which always showed her joy, she commented with calm assurance, "He'll do. . . . He'll do!"

19th February

I am finding peace. I am at peace. I am absorbed into the atmosphere of peace. I have found tranquillity to the measure in which I can accept and appreciate it. I no longer need to strive and struggle, as I did in the earth life. Always there I worked too hard. I strove. I battled forward. I followed every channel, every path which seemed to lead to that 'break-through' of the spirit for which my soul yearned so deeply. I obeyed the precepts, followed the doctrines, studied and examined all theories which could 'explain' the spirit; drove myself with the whip of an iron will, read, marked, digested the sciences (so called) of the human mind and its reactions to stimuli, as well as the human psyche and its reaching forward into revelation. All this with a great purpose, as I supposed, of Illumination. I strove always for the 'break-through' to spirit, union with the soul, contact with the Great Forces, and always, driving my mind and my personal will was the hope, the glory, the bliss of a 'break-through' to spirit. And now as I look back over my earth life, I realise that so much was illusion.

I sought the Spirit and the Spirit was there all the time.

"He came unto His own and His own received Him not."

As I rest now in this Reality I see, with sadness, the truth of those words. *I knew Him not.* I struggled, fasted, sought for what was already present, perfect and everlasting within me. Like most of us in the body life I was in illusion; lost in glamour. I looked for the Spirit to reveal itself to me, when all that was necessary was 'relaxation unto God'. The Spirit was always with me, veiled because physical sight could not view it. The great secret of finding that Spirit was the 'letting go' of self. I, who longed so much for the touch of the divine, who dedicated my life to religious work, who read lives of the saints for their examples, who delved into the sciences of psychology, extrasensory perception and all psychic phenomena, as well as into the occult sciences, who denied myself the usual sensual and reproductive life of a human being; who truly tried to obey the precepts of the Master, as related in the New Testament, I had not accepted the simple Reality of those words: "Behold, I am with you even unto the end". I had not been able to let go, and let the Spirit absorb me. As I now see my thoughts, actions, aspirations from this angle, I am realising that the very tenseness of my striving was my undoing and it barred the way to that very union for which my soul longed. I battered at the Veil which hid the Face of Divinity trying by my mind and will to tear it away, the more intense my thought, the more real did I create the illusion. For the Veil was, as I now realise, the Veil of my own setting.

Light, Divinity, Reality . . . all-pervading consciousness . . . were there for my *acceptance*. Much greater progress would have been made by 'letting go' of all these human images and by allowing the spirit to absorb me. Relax and allow the Spirit to stream through you. Swim with the tide of the Spirit. That is the great lesson I am learning here as I review my mistakes. Now I am 'in the Spirit'. . . . There was no 'break-through' to Spirit, of which I once, so glibly talked. There is only a gradual absorption of that amount, or degree of Spirit which the openness of the soul can accept. This degree, as I appreciate now, must be governed by the Law of Progress, for the Spirit is never limited, only ourselves, as receptacles, govern the degree of its entrance.

This is indeed a salutary lesson.

I am aware too that in the last life experience I but repeated old struggles. None of it was new. No adventure into matter, into the exterior, is ever entirely fresh or untried. It has all been worked to its end perhaps hundreds of times before, though under different circumstances, perhaps in different worlds. I can not be sure of that yet; and it will be worked again and again until we, as souls, learn to 'carry the Light' with us, through our personalities.

Freewill, the development of the logical mind, the illusions of the senses, all these tend to extinguish, or at least, to dim, the Light of Divinity. Now I perceive more clearly, for I am no longer cluttered by illusions, that the great purpose of life in matter is *to illumine matter with Spirit*.

Even here, in my new life, I have been rushing hither and thither in search of adventure, of experience, of progress and such as I have discovered I have tried to relate in my account.

But now, I let go. I seek for nothing. I absorb and am absorbed by the Spirit of Light, Love, Beauty. I know that I am being remade. Consciousness is expanding to acknowledge and accept the fact of being a Child of the Living Light, of already having, in consciousness, all that is needed and reflecting as much of the Spirit as my awareness will permit.

Life still goes on about me. The work of helping others who may be also bogged down in their illusions of separativeness still occupies me and is a joy. I no longer crave to pass on to the next stage, that of being allowed to be a student in the outer courts of the Universities here. Such glorious adventure will be mine when my consciousness is ready for it. Until such awareness is alive and active in me and I have achieved the maintenance of the deep tranquillity of this knowledge, I am content to remain here, and to benefit by the loving atmosphere.

Until this new peace has become an integrated part of me, until all old regrets have been dissolved in love and service, until I have learned to rest completely in this new consciousness of the Spirit, I shall remain where I am. Time, as we reckoned it, does not exist here. Consciousness has taken its place. By the degree of consciousness of the Spirit can we measure the extent of, the habitation of, varying states in our onward progress. To you still in the concept of time, this could be months, years, centuries. For me now the state of consciousness of living Spirit and the serenity such consciousness works in my soul, is my present and my future in this Life Everlasting.

25th February

I have changed, and yet I have not changed. My mind is

still the same, eager and thirsting for knowledge as when I was in the third dimension of earth life, only now the frontiers of revelation are open and welcoming, avenues of research lead into domains of the Spirit which, even in my most aspiring dreams, had never manifested themselves. I am free, as far as my progress will allow, and believe me, the barriers are in one's own consciousness, to pursue my explorations into the nature of Eternity. The only hindrances to progress are from one's limited reception of Light. I can only liken this to the transmission of electricity. Intenser electric light and power need greater voltage; greater voltage requires thicker cables of connecting wires. One must have developed the 'thicker cable' with all the leads-in united and 'plugged in'. With cables of lesser voltage there will be lesser light, it is as simple as that.

For the exploration to which I can look forward with sure joy I must clear my lines of all the old faults and errors. I have to develop within me more 'lines of communication' more 'wire transmissions' to increase the voltage. For these reasons and anticipations I am content to meditate upon past mistakes and to see how they can be reconciled into the Pattern as well as to learn lessons of incarnation from the stories of those who come to us here. And with it all, life and service here fill everything with joy and I am finding an exciting approach to truth. There are always those who have travelled further into Reality to whom to turn for instruction and advice. There is beauty in its fullness, there is freedom of soul, and there is the wonderful realisation that I am the same, that I who was also masked and belaboured by the egoism of the personality, am changed and yet not changed. The essential remains. The unessentials are slowly being stripped away so that the joy of the Spirit remains, and an abiding peace.

"In my Father's House are many Mansions. . . ."

This temporary dwellingplace of the Spirit is my rightful 'mansion' now. But what joy to know—as well as to anticipate —other mansions for further states of living!

This is the message which I desire, so much, to put through this work.

After the death of the physical body we gravitate to our rightful place; a mansion, a cottage, even a hovel, as we have earned. It is essential therefore to regard life experience, whilst in incarnation on the earth plane as a *preparation* for this existence. *Live Life in Eternity Now.*

Someone once said: "Live each day as if it was your last". There is great wisdom in this, for the knowledge will transform thought and action into positivity and reality, bypassing the glamour of earth life and bringing the incarnation nearer to the original Plan, thus preparing the abode here in the Light of the Christ Love. By deeper understanding of these precepts, the soul's communion with the personality will become closer, the less will the persona be allowed to be an obstacle to the soul's pattern, the more valuable and useful will the current incarnation be, and the greater the progress of the soul.

25th February—Later

The Band and I have not been able to touch your mind in these last sessions easily due to the unevenness of your whole vibratory pattern. This factor is caused by the temporary ill-health of your body. You recall that I told you, and how surprised and critical you were, that I was not able to meditate whilst I was in those last difficult weeks of my body illness? Well, it was true, and now you see for yourself how the Light seemed to have been withdrawn from you during your own feelings of weakness and sickness. It is as if there has been a power cut in the electricity supply. Because the body entities are so real to us in our earth life, and because, as yet, most of us are not sufficiently advanced to supersede this body-call, we are cut off from the High Supply. The vibrations slow down—become grounded in matter—become denser and harder to penetrate.

9th March

I see that you have been reading Dr. Weatherhead's book *The Christian Agnostic.* I particularly noticed that you paused and reread the following passage:

'Unless we can break out of the prison of old-fahioned expressions, creeds and formulae, we shall never be free to find the far more glorious truths which are inherent in the Christian religion.'

As you know, from my life story, I dedicated myself to the religious life and, after years of repeating these creeds and forms with my lips, years during which my will was stretched and exerted to keep me honourably performing to the best of my ability those vows which I had so solemnly made, after twenty-five years of such devotion to my religion, I found myself unable to go on any longer.

Not that I no longer believed in God, or did not care to follow the pattern of Jesus, nor that I doubted that Christ was the Light of the World, but because, into my experience and thoughts had seeped, to me, a new explanation of these mysteries. Personal discovery had implanted within me doubts of the veracity of those tenets of the Faith which even more than twenty years ago were being superseded as outmoded, limited in interpretation, and impractical forms for modern belief.

Now, in this new World to which I am gradually being introduced with all its beauty and light and freedom, I can look back with joy that such a step was part of my experience. For I have not, like so many good and conventional souls, arrived here with thought and expectation coloured by old half-truths; with prejudices against survival of the personality as well as of the soul to be dissolved, albeit painfully, in this new expression of freedom. At least I am thankful to relate, I came in expectation, in anticipation, in utter belief of a new life, and thus I found joy in the reunion of old contacts, as well as delight in obeying the Law of recompense and of service. I passed through the experience of death firmly believing in the Resurrection, but not of the body that clothed me on earth. How could I ever desire to bring an old, worn-out thing into this new Life? Or ever to occupy it again at any future experience.

Here I have a body, certainly, but it is of finer composition than my late physical body. Here I look as I did on earth, or relatively as I looked, but here I am free to refashion this body by thought. I am beginning that adventure of breaking out of the prison of those creeds which limited the reality of life. Here I dwell temporarily amongst my fellow religious in a community which is entirely dedicated to helping souls to awaken to greater freedom before they proceed onwards to their 'rightful places', and to the extent in which I am allowed to participate, I am learning more and more of the true values of each soul's experience in all the worlds through which it is destined to pass in its progress towards Divinity.

There are no tenets, no creeds, no formulae, no hard and fast rules devised by any mind to restrict or confine progress here. All is individual, and yet all is for the good of the whole; for the advancement of the group. It is a 'forward and backward' movement, if I may be allowed to use a contradictory expression. Each soul and each group moves onward towards greater expansion, towards the Divine conception of an illimitable Creation, individually and collectively. Yet at the same time each group and each soul directs 'backward' to the plane below, its present achievement, the fruits of its knowledge. These ideas, ideals and conceptions fit into and make manifest, the Divine Pattern or Plan as far as this can be accepted by the souls still seeped in the illusion and glamour of matter. No acceptance of another soul's belief colours progress. The soul must judge for itself—must make its own progress, must choose what to accept as truth for itself. No soul is coerced, forced or bound by creeds. If he believes that this is Heaven, or conversely, that he is in Hell, then for him *that is so at his present state of progress*.

Helpers and Teachers and Great Souls there are in number to explain such errors of thinking, but there are no rules to follow and obey except the Divine Precept of Love, Light, Wisdom and Understanding.

Jesus said: "I am the Light of the World" and truly He had found and could live in that Light. We are striving to live also in that Light as *it presents itself as truth to us individually*. This is the glory of the Christian religion, as of all religions; this inner stamp of Divinity in each soul, whether blinded and deafened by material thinking or not. Our 'inner eyes' are opened gradually or swiftly to the errors of our old patterns of thinking and acting. We are allowed to progress into such experiences as will help us to put right these errors. In some, this means remaining in one state until the effects of the disasters of their actions in earth lives have been resolved and love and harmony have healed the hurts. For others, this means joining a Group where the omissions in their thinking and feeling can be remedied. Yet still for others there is service to their fellows, whilst to those happy few advanced souls there is swift progress to other and higher spheres.

The 'serial life' from one plane to another, from one experience to another, from one group to another, from one adventure to another, from partial understanding to deeper comprehension, from apparent separation to inherent unity and on into the bliss of Divine Reality, that seems to me, as far as I have progressed, and as clearly as my growing understanding has shown me, to be the 'glorious truths', as Dr. Weatherhead says, of the Christian, or any other religion, which emphasises the here and the hereafter.

11th March

You must not think that the Community in which I now sojourn is the same religious community of which I became a member when on earth. Many of the Sisters are here as of old; there are others also from similar communities. Many have passed on to greater activities; others are as new and 'recent' as my own arrival. The term recent I am using in a purely metaphorical way for already my experience of earth and time is fading. I seem to have been here for aeons. Already the sharp edge to emotions which made certain events stand forth clearly in one's memory, is dissolving in the expiation of the effects of my actions. I begin to correlate life as a whole now so that different periods dovetail into the Pattern and the Pattern becomes related to the Whole. This Community differs from the earth Community in that we have no creeds, no restrictions, no vows (except that of self-dedication of service to our fellows) and no ranks of seniority. We are one in service. We are individual in thought and progress. Ceremony we still perform, in a fuller and wider sense, for there is ever a need for the upliftment of the soul by dedicated and meaningful action correlated with intense thought and aspiration.

Yet these 'ceremonials' are not of the pattern prescribed as on earth. Here our ceremonies spring from an innate oneness with the Source of all Life, an eagerness to participate, a welling upwards of the Life Force in us so as to initiate a mingling with one another as well as with the greater Forces. Here, and in other places, I have taken part in what we call *the Ceremony of Light*. This formation of thought, this deep concerted concentration, springs from the deep desire to experience Life and yet more Life, to unite with the Supreme Essence, to realise as far as one's present consciousness will allow that Life is *expansion*, that Light is but the widening of one's inner perceptions. Such ceremonies and festivals seem to be for the purpose of breaking down barriers which obstruct those lingering inhibitions of the personality which circumscribe the soul and which have to be consciously dissolved and discarded before Light can truly flow in. In these Festivals of Light there is a 'raising up into' Power and Energy rather than a 'pouring down'.

As one takes one's place amongst the Community of Souls making this observance of ceremony, one is conscious of a supreme quickening of tempo, a heightening of the action of the dynamo of the Spirit. There is a distinct feeling of growth; the body seems to expand, to become less gross, to stretch into a new elasticity and ethereal content. The mind soars to a hitherto unexplored vastness of creative activity. The Spirit fills all with a dynamic lift of consciousness. New and vast concepts stream into the mind. The onward Path is illumined with a clarity that surpasses all imagination.

"This is Truth" one whispers, awed yet exhilarated. "This is Light."

These festivals are accompanied, as always in ceremony, with music on a grander scale than anything that is performed on earth. Yet have I never 'seen' instruments such as were necessary for the production of such harmonies on earth. The notes form and are trilled as though by some unseen performers. There is no dissonance, but a growing ascendancy of some majestic theme; there is a swelling of harmony until a particular chord or note is reached and held. That note seems to be the key, the aim, the object of the ceremony. All movements, all voices raised in unison, all sounds from the Spheres unite in experiment until the ascension of the right note, rather in the manner of a birdchorus at dawn, lifting gently into a grand finale with every bird throat pouring forth its contribution of sound.

Here, the Note, when at last reached and sounded in full, is held and *vibrated* at a pitch of intensity which sweeps every soul into harmony. Then Light breaks through into the assembly. Light surrounds us, lifts us, touches us, awakens us. One finds oneself expressing, or trying to express, the Note with all of one's mind and all feeling and intensity of which one is capable. One is singing, and yet not singing, with one voice, as in earthly choirs. *One is singing with the whole organism.*

Thought, production, feeling, expression, aspiration and exaltation become united in one vast effort to capture and hold in consciousness that Note, *to live in and become the vibration of that Ray of Light expressed through the sounding Note.*

It is the ascendancy of the Light.

It is union with the vast Worlds of Spirit.

It is the impregnation of matter with Spiritual Force.

It is the Light Universal, the Light of which Christ spoke when He said: "I am the Light of the World".

It is the Light of all the Worlds . . . of this world, of the physical world as well as of all higher, vaster Worlds. . . .

It is the Light that penetrates and becomes Essence in us.

It is Sound, Harmony and Light in One.

This is the Ceremony of Light!

When I was in the Community on earth, I loved the Ceremony of the Eucharist. Yet now I realise how pale are the festivals and ceremonies performed with the *separated* consciousness of the human mind. Yet these ceremonies are of value for they engender uplifting aspirations. The value, as I now see it, in ceremony is in the participator's *intensity* of application; the intent with which the ritual is performed and followed.

On earth I had little ear for music. I believe that I explained in my book *Frontiers of Revelation* that all my impressions of other 'states' were visual. I rarely 'heard'. More often I saw or was aware of vibration about the physical bodies of my companions. Here I am learning to achieve both the Eye and the Ear of Light . . . to see the Light as well as to hear the vibrations of the different frequencies of Light.

14th March

Perhaps the most important change which has come over me in the period since I left the earth, is the deepening of the realisation and confirmation of the *serialised* life which we all lead. It is as though I had just finished a chapter, put down my pen, closed the book and slept for very weariness. . . . Now I am awake, refreshed, alert and I have started immediately on a new chapter, or perhaps it is a new book in a different dimension. It does not matter whether this is a new book or only a new chapter. It is still a continuation, a sequel to all that has been committed to memory in the last story. There is a definite *continuing thread*. One meets old friends, tried companions, and former Teachers. From conversations and communions with them, and through listening to their stories, the missing portions of one's own experiences return to memory, and the pattern is built up anew. Not that the pattern of the continued life was ever completely lost. As the chief actor in my own particular drama I had become, as it were, so immersed in the last act or chapter that the incidents, tragedies, lessons of the previous scenes had tended to grow misty. But now I am beginning slowly and laboriously to piece together these scenes into a whole, into a serialised effort at living. Many of the incidents which have been jogged back into my memory by the confrontation of its co-actors long obscured in my consciousness come as a shock to me. Could this have been how I thought, spoke, acted? What great similarity there is in all the acts, yet how different! The Essence is steady and serene; the persona changing and elusive. As I meditate upon some flash of memory, some bead on the chain of experiences either on this plane, the earth plane or some other plane, the Plan unfolds itself, only partially of course, to my fascinated gaze. Did I pass up this great chance? Did I respond in such a puerile way? Did I not learn to listen to those vague memory flashes that spoke to me from time to time during all the experiences which 'separatist' thinking often turned into escapades? Had I sunk so far into matter that I had forgotten lessons already learned, philosophies so often established, as Real to my mind?

Truly I must have. The comparisons fill me with dismay. Can I give an illustration?

I have had the wonderful illumination of being transported by thought, temporarily, to a Plane where I was in contact with a great Soul, a Sage, an Advanced One, a Teacher of Wisdom Who is one of the Divine Company. His Face flashed into sight before me. I knew Him. There was no need for speech.

In the manner of this new dimension to which I am becoming accustomed, I understood in silence all that He was communicating to me. It was as if my journeys were unrolled before me on a screen of colour and movement, yet without sound. I was entranced and at times joyful, sad, proud and ashamed.

Yet He never uttered a word of blame. He smiled with infinite understanding as, once again, only this time on a vaster and more detailed scale, the Blueprint showed with definite markings, the little triumphs as well as the failures of my endeavours.

"I am, I was, I always shall be"—I recall thinking. As if in answer I saw Him—in flashes—as He was when I had contacted Him in my various states of Being, for He had played a part in many experiences and always as the Brother, the Mentor, the Inspirer.

"And I knew Him not" I thought with sadness. "I remembered Him not."

As I looked again at Him I saw that His Face was the Face of infinite limitless Love. In my inner 'ear' sounded the words "Neither do I condemn thee". . . . I was suffused with new joy, great hope and a deep strength of consciousness. I was so moved that I found myself weeping inwardly. And when I recovered myself the vision was gone and I was back in my garden, contemplating the glory of Life Eternal and the Way of endless possibilities.

Mother Florence was beside me.

"You knew all this?" I asked.

"I too forgot when in the earth body" she answered with her usual gentleness.

"But you achieved so much" I persisted.

"I also failed."

"You too have seen Him?" I asked.

Her face was radiant. "I have met such as He when I have been allowed to visit Higher Planes."

"Met Them?" I marvelled, almost in reproof I added "And yet you choose to remain here?"

"Choose." She considered this. "I have a duty, dear Sister, and my own expiation which also is my choice. Besides," she explained, "I do not believe that I could stand, for long, the intense Light and Glory of these Higher Planes. My soul is not yet strong enough."

I was silenced. Without even a hint of reproof I had been

made to realise a fault in myself. How much I need to learn. How divine is true humility.

But "neither do I condemn thee".

The words echo in my thought like a bursting bud of great promise. The Way is eternal. Our little minds are illumined and comforted with the knowledge that the 'serial life' is a wonderfully kind project of Divine Compassion for each of us. As we have tried to achieve in other consciousnesses, other states of Being, so will we be allowed to go on, chapter by chapter, serial by serial, book by book, to grow in wisdom and beauty into that image so gloriously represented, that of the Divine Image. I am filled with hope, with serenity and with tranquil acceptance even in the contemplation of such progress in the far distant scheme of things.

25th March

I mentioned that I would talk about Groups and the subject that was very close to our hearts when I was in incarnation, that of the Group Soul.

Nothing that has occurred here or has been shown to me in the occurrences of my life here in Eternity has brought any change in my belief in Group Work and in the evidence of Group Souls . . . or if you care to express in another way, Soul Groups which unite to constitute a Group Soul. This concept, I am perfectly aware, will not fit in with much of the theology of the established Churches of Christendom. Nor will it be acceptable to many people, due to an inherent, cultivated idea of man's individual importance, in other words, people object to being, as they choose to term it, only a cell in a great conglomeration of cells, a soul in a group formation of souls. Yet why should they? What proof has anyone that he or she is a single and isolated unit of Life? The whole of nature expresses the unity of the Life Plan, plants, animals, minerals belong to different *families*, and respond uniformly to prescribed patterns.

Should the human then be so different?

Since my life began here, my eyes have been opened to the great and wise Truths inherent in these concepts of Groups. And as the world is now going into a new Age, with new conceptions, this question of Group Souls will come to be more and more postulated, even by those who now prefer to discern pride in the isolation of units.

We are, to my limited knowledge, all members not of one Group but of many, and the many make up the Great Group or the Great Soul Being in which we live and move and have our being ... and these great Beings unite to form further great Group Souls or Divine Beings in the Divine Company of Heaven. This is possibly a difficult concept to take at first, but I will try and break it down for those who are interested to read these ideas.

(1) First of all we belong to a Family Group. We are born into and marry into, Family Groups, which are most suitable for the type of experience and lessons we, as incarnating souls, need. Many people do not get far away from the Family Groups or Tribes (in lesser cultivated nations). The Family Group Soul is the most important in their lives. They are the folk we call clannish. Naturally when they arrive over here after death of the physical body they graduate to that Family Group there to carry on the lessons and experiences of earth life, and develop harmony and happiness. There is no compulsion for them to leave the Group until they are ready and willing to go on to the next larger Group to which they, all unwittingly, also belong. This first is the simplest Group and many souls remain under the joyful protection and guidance of this Group Being for a long span.

(2) The next Groups are the Groups of interest, passionate attachments to the arts, music, education, social sciences and social service. These are wider, more extensive Groups and extend beyond families and individuals to smaller groups. Such Groups would be those of musicians, artists, prophets, orators, writers, doctors, philosophers, scientists who had passed through the Group Work and had graduated. Their passionate interest would naturally be part of their soul life and they would graduate to such groups where they could continue their studies and their achievements. Sometimes Family Groups are included in these larger groups and then the two groups fit into one another and merge. In other words, these Family Groups would be as cells within the Higher Mental Groups.

When souls arrive here and have 'cleared the receiving

houses' they pass on to, first, the Family and then later (if the family is not of similar mental groups) to the Special Group of their interests. This is rather like 'clearing customs' on earth, at arrival in a new country, then joining the family awaiting your arrival and later, passing on to your business or mental or artistic associates. The groups fit in with one another, or are part of one another, just as the finger is part of the hand, the hand of the arm, and the arm of the body.

(3) The next stage of groups is on a higher level and is not always attained by souls who desire rapid return to earth conditions. To me, in my humble state now in my first group (that of interest and service as in the Community on earth), the probability of being included in these Higher Groups of extended consciousness is a joyful anticipation towards which I work gladly, yet with contented assent.

We could compare these Higher Groups with the advanced classes in a university. Here the interests, the subjects for study are still partially separated. The advanced student is accepted into classes of wider range, power and interest. In the guidance of these Groups are great Beings, watching over the progress of their cell-like clusters of souls. They work on higher mental Rays of influence, for although I know very little about them as yet, I have questioned many souls who have contacted them and worked amongst them. These Soul Groups are extensive, yet concentrated in their classes and workshops. They realise more than we can possibly do the Divinity inherent in every particle of the Cosmos. They are able to study Divine Laws beyond our understanding. They commune together *with* and *in* the Mind of the Higher Beings whose Soul Group they constitute. They work for progress in Divine Imagination and they work as Divine Imaginational Groups. They inspire lower groups with their findings, for still they *contain* the lower groups within their Centres as cell-points in a vast intricate and beautiful organism.

Amongst them are philosophers, scientists, researchers, priests, teachers. They are parts of Groups which influence and impress such movements on earth as Psychic Research, Healing movements, Religious Co-operation, the advancement of Science and all movements intended to bring Light upon future worlds.

When I am ready and my 'cleansing' and 'sloughing off of earthly desires' has advanced sufficiently for me to be enabled to live in a rarer atmosphere, I trust that I shall move on to take up habitation and study in one of these Groups. Then I shall be able to attend the classes and listen to the Teachers and discuss with my fellows in one of these Universities of the Spirit. Then I shall be able to take part in the communion with the Great Spiritual Being who is the Centre of the Group. But this is to come.

(4) Beyond these Groups there must be other Groups and Companies of Heaven, Greater Beings, vaster projects right up to the concept of Divinity Itself, of which we can have little or no conception.

I have not mentioned the Shadow Lands here because, to my mind, these seem to be the clearing houses where unlawful and mischievous adjuncts of the old personalities are rejected, discarded and finally resolved. At this particular place in my own progress I am in my own 'interest' group, that of the Community and service, but I am also aware of the Group beyond to which I belong and to which I trust I am gravitating. I have already contacted briefly some of those who dwell in those wider Spheres, and I am able to communicate through the inner thought and to receive impressions from them. As a point of interest I will reiterate that which I told you before. These scripts are organised and impressed upon me by a Band of Souls. Thus I am being used as a telepathic link to you and to the earth by these Souls.

This Group then is the next stage for me to which I look forward with joyful anticipation. I shall still be a part of the Community and I shall be able to return here whenever I wish for service and refreshment but I shall also be absorbed into the Higher Group. It is always easier of course to step back into a former group than it is to progress on into the atmosphere of groups of wider consciousness until one is completely ready. I shall therefore be connected with these two groups as well as my Family Group which I have not mentioned here as it is personal to me.

Can you appreciate now what I mean by Group Work and Group Souls? One group is within another, within the next and the next into the highest Beam of Light which is Divine Life Itself—or God. All is progress. Nothing is static. Imagination passes and grows from the emotional to the mental to the spiritual levels. Life is a continuing Path towards one's particular Group, one's individual experiences, one's own progress and onwards into the arc of ascendancy. To me this is a far more heartening process than any glory of a static heaven with angels and golden floors.

Angels, of course, there are; great Beings of Light who do the Will of the Divine Creator and who carry and transmit Power and Beauty and Light. But they too are in the process of progress, advancement towards their own great Centres. All is order, advancement, progress. And all is unity. Life cells within Life cells, centres within Centres, Groups within Groups, into the very Heart of Divinity.

28th March—More about Groups

I said that we belong to groups, one within another, such as groups of family, interests, absorbing work, aspirations, creeds, etc. That is true and that the Group Soul or Group Spirit is the Being in whom the members of the Group live and move. In other words His is the Fount of Divine Life and Energy from which the Groups draws its inspiration, its life, its intuitions.

To tune in, therefore, to the Life, Power and Beauty of such a Group Spirit is to experience the God Power within one's own mind and soul. All great aspirations, revelations and divine whisperings of intuition originate in and through the Spirit of the Group to which one belongs, i.e. the Highest Point of the Group. Thus, family sacrifices, family peace, love, harmony all originate from the Group Soul of the family; in the same way, great aspirations for service and for imparting knowledge to others and for the guiding and enlightenment of our fellows, comes from the Great Spiritual Being who is the Centre Group Spirit of that particular Group.

Since I left the earth life I have been taught by a Teacher with whom I am in contact, mentally and spiritually. He Himself is a part of the Group Soul in the Group towards which I am progressing and of which, although I was not entirely aware, I have been a member for many ages. This Teacher is a higher Disciple, a wise and advanced soul, and is able to impart knowledge and wisdom to souls in the Group. Here, *progress, when made, is always rewarded with a service.* In other words, as one advances to greater Light, so one is allowed to teach and guide others of the Group on a lesser path. The Group itself is made up of souls at all levels of consciousness, from the highest to the mediocre, but the Spirit of the Groups only Itself advances as the younger and less knowledgeable members make progress. It is a unified advance. No member of the Group can pass beyond the call and communication of other members. When the Group itself advances into the Divine Company, then there will be no 'stragglers'. But, as I am instructed, such an experience is far beyond the Group consciousness at this stage.

You too belong to this same Group. Indeed you might be surprised to learn of the personalities in the smaller groups which are all banded together to form the great Group. It embraces many other apparently separate groups.

Thus we are indeed 'one with another' and it seems to me that one of our chief lessons to learn whilst immersed in the personality is that of *tolerance*. For often we do not know (how can we when our eyes are veiled in the earthly life?) who is a member of our same group. We may even feel a sense of repellance towards a certain person, even though he appears to be working along identical lines of thought with us, but repellance is shallow, ephemeral and later, when we have shed some of the lesser aspects of the personality, we may find that the other person is an advanced member of our own Group to whom we are indissolubly linked by ties of spiritual kinship.

On the other hand there are souls to whom we instinctively and immediately react with affection, admiration, union. I used to believe that these were souls with whom we had been in contact in other incarnations and to whom we owed karmic debts or who owed us reparation for wrongs inflicted. Now my understanding is widening. What I believed may still be true in part, but now I realise that those souls who attract us are *part of ourselves*. They belong to the same Group, the same Spiritual Family, the same Group Soul. Their connection with us is deeper and far more permanent than mere earth contacts could make it. They may be part of the same Spirit as that Spirit is Itself part of the Great Spirit, the great Company of Divinity, far beyond our comprehension, the Company of Heaven, the Co-Creators, the Divine and Beautiful Sons of God.

I am learning much, experiencing much, comprehending

more. I realised that on earth I tried too hard, I worked too *strongly*, I essayed too much. Now I am learning to absorb through *experience* and not entirely through *mental application*, although the application of the mind attributes will ever be part of my make-up. The mental activity was a part of my lesser self. It was not the Essence of which I am slowly becoming aware, slowly and perhaps of my ignorance, painfully absorbing. Painfully. That may have a strange connotation but a deep significance. Yet with the pain of regret for opportunity neglected, there is still the deep joy of the spirit for greater realisation, which is Light itself.

"Let go . . . and let the Spirit flow into you" was one of the teachings of Plotinus, and how true he was. One does not need to *strive* for perfection. Let the perfection of the soul and spirit seep through the windows and doors of the personality.

You recall how much I loved Francis Thompson's 'Hound of Heaven'? What a deeply spiritual insight was in the mind of the poet. He wrote of the Light pursuing us down the years, down the Ages, I would add. It, the Light, the Spirit, the Highest Aspect of any Group Soul is part of us in every incarnation, every existence, in all our wanderings from Heaven, in all our experiences. It is the Divine Group Spirit, the extension of God, the Fountain and Head which, by our endeavours, poor though they may be, evolves ever inwards to the eternal Centre of Light and Creative Energy which men call God. In this progressive creation, by Groups and Companies, we progress onwards and upwards into that Divine Self, after aeons of endeavour, into inclusion in the Divine Company, into bliss which is inexplicable at our present stage of understanding.

The Spirit of Life is far more wonderful, more awe-inspiring, more glorious and far extending than man has ever realised. In the flight of the eagle we can watch the bird soar up into the sky, we can distinguish the beat and whirl of its wings, we discern its progress, until it becomes but a speck in the heavens, and soars beyond our following. That is Life itself, only visible and but partially understood at its lowest level, and lost to us as it presses ever onwards to join the limitless sky of God's Creative Love.

3rd April

I am getting to the end of my work for this book now. The scripts will not be so long and arduous though I may still be instructed to add more from time to time.

When I first came here and 'awoke' to this new and free life without the drawbacks of my physical body, I was thrilled and excited. I longed to rush it all to you who had been my partner in so many thrilling spiritual adventures at the end of my sojourn. I knew instantly that I could contact you by the telepathic methods which we had been studying. I wanted to write all my experiences, describe the people I met, the cases at which I was allowed to assist and detail every bit of my life here to you. And so I did. I thought I was doing this on my own, until I learned that I was an instrument of a greater Group. That too was a thrill, to realise that our Group Work had been a preparation for this means of contact. I threw myself into the work and service here with greater joy. I pondered long upon the 'cases' which I had described to you. I began to comprehend more and more the wonder and reality of this 'serial' life.

This then is the message which we want to put across before I finish the scripts:

(1) There should be no fear of death, for the death of the body is but a gentle passing to a much freer life.

(2) That all Life is lived as a serial, that we go from one experience of living to another experience of living at a different rate, i.e. on a higher level of awareness.

(3) That much of what we thought praiseworthy on earth is mediocre to us in the Light of wider knowledge, and conversely much for which we blamed ourselves and were blamed by others, is viewed here from a wider angle and even becomes merit! That sounds like a contradictory statement, yet it makes sense when viewed from this freer angle.

Now I am calm. I have settled down and am fast becoming adjusted to this new life, enjoying the love and service with many I knew on earth, teaching those who find difficulty in adjustment, and in absorbing the Essence of Beauty and Light in which we dwell. There is infinite hope, later, of going onwards and of joining the greater Group to which I have always belonged . . . the Group which contains this Group also in its Spiritual Consciousness.

But I am content and happy in the work to which my talents, such as they are, and the mental training I underwent on earth, can be applied. The Group is satisfied with the way in which the scripts have been transmitted and received. Such small errors as there have been will be adjusted, or will be of little matter, and I trust the book resulting will be of help to many souls on earth. It is only a preparatory pamphlet for I am still only in the preparatory stage of my journey. But it will serve, and by so doing, will thrice bless us all, to open minds of many to this new life towards which every human being is travelling, and if it makes plainer the answers to a few of the questions which have plagued those still in incarnation on earth, our task will have been well and truly done.

Blessings upon you and upon all who read this humble testimony of the Light of the Spirit and the Spirit of Life.

14th April

[Helen Greaves)]

A feeling of great and abiding peace came upon me. I remember that it was a chill April day with snow showers and the electricity supply failed in the morning, so that for the best part of the day I was without heat, except for a faithful old oil stove. The light was bad and I was trying to type out a talk to be given before the weekend. There were many physical difficulties and annoyances. . . . Suddenly the wave of peace swept over me. I folded my hands and let myself be absorbed into its beauty and repose. The Spirit, as it were, seeped into me like soft light, warmth and radiance. I felt very well, very calm, yet very alert and with an inward tranquillity that seemed beyond explanation.

"This is the Spirit" I told myself, opening to it like a light-starved plant to the sunshine. "This is Spirit."

Gently, imperceptibly, I became aware of Frances. She was influencing my mind and, quite distinctly, I 'registered' the thoughts she was conveying to me. Indeed, as soon as I let myself 'listen' the thoughts formed into words and without a moment's hesitation I reached for my pen. . . .

[Frances]

I can use my 'inner Mind' so much more now [Francis wrote through my pen and mind]. On earth it was difficult to 'break through' to Spirit for long enough periods to be lasting in effect. I tried, by meditation, and I did succeed in stilling the conscious mind, but I did not then achieve a measure of living in the Spiritual Mind, as I am now able to do. Yes, I still have several 'parts' or 'bodies' and I marvel more as I recognise them. The 'purely personal' part of me is being cleansed and purified. I live mostly now in an astral body and that gives a measure of greater freedom than a dense physical body, but I am very aware of my Higher Body, or if you wish, my inner self, much more aware of it than when in incarnation in the physical plane of matter. I am now learning, and achieving I trust, a higher balance of living. By this I mean that I am becoming aware of my Spiritual Body and in so doing I am enabled to absent myself from this plane of thought, the astral or emotional, and slip-away in consciousness to the higher Mental and Spiritual planes of thought.

With the transition from this consciousness to that of the Higher comes an exquisite sense of peace and freedom such as I can scarcely explain.

[Here, I Helen Greaves, asked mentally if the peace I had felt so recently was a sample of this sense.]

Yes, but only a fraction of its intensity. I cannot hope even to transmit the enveloping peace, the sense of tranquil being that envelopes one with this transition of consciousness. It is the break-through for which I longed when on earth and which I only experienced in infinitesimal moments of Union. It is the Reality of Being. It is joy beyond words. It is in truth an ecstasy of living, of being a live, alert Self in a world of Live and Glorious Selves within a consciousness of a Great Creative Self. I cannot express this feeling of Inner Spirit more clearly. And I must add that I am but a tyro yet in achieving even this measure of consciousness. Neither can I hold it indefinitely at my present stage of evolution. Perhaps the intensity of it would, so to speak, burn me up until I am attuned to this stepped-up frequency of vibration. It is intense joy, unqualified bliss, the aim and acme of all the struggles to discover the Spirit, and still only can I achieve it in 'periods' of consciousness. Yet I can be content as I become more fully alert to the possibilities of the Higher Planes.

15th April

I am like a creature hibernating, and yet at the same time, sloughing off a skin which I no longer will be needing. I feel, sometimes, like a snake gradually shedding its skin. These coils of lower density are slipping away from me. I am emerging from regrets of earth memories, from disillusions, from idealisations which become illusions, ephemeral and of no true worth. I am viewing each piece of skin which peels off from me in its right connection with the true Self which it served to obscure. And more and more I become thankful for the Reality which, God be praised, was there beneath the skin, all the time. This is the Self which is now becoming more and more outstanding, more revealed, more substantial. That Self is substantial Light. Perhaps that last sentence rings oddly to you. I am trying not to become obscure, but one's angle of vision alters on this plane of living. I realise that what is passing from me, like sloughing a skin, is insubstantial, impermanent, decomposing, as it drops from me into a dusty nothingness. What is left is essentially Light, is Reality, is permanent and is true. I call this my new Body of Light and that, indeed, is what it truly is. A Body of Light, not dense and material and dull and heavy as the physical body, not insubstantial, shadowy and unreal as the astral body in which I have been sheltering, but brilliant, 'encelled' with Light, ethereal in that there is no weight, no dragging down into matter but is enmeshed with colour and beauty into form and substance. Is that a difficult conception? You must remember that I am forming this, my spiritual Body, or should I be more correct in saying I am merging into it. That sounds a paradox but then much to which I am becoming adjusted here is paradoxical when viewed in the light of the restricted thinking of the human mind. I still have a mind, I still have a body, but both are inevitably changing and because of that I feel as if I am emerging, like a grub from a chrysalis, to a butterfly. Gradually I can function more readily and for deeper periods in my Body of Light, and in it, can commune with more advanced Souls and imbibe their wisdom.

16th April

I am trying to function more and more in this Body of Light. I cannot sustain it for long yet, but I have the joy and bliss of the certainty of a further expansion which is available to us all. This is the next step in progression, the stepping out of illusion into the consciousness of the functioning of the Higher Self, an emergence into a wider consciousness and an awareness of Spiritual Beings and of Forces from the All-Creative Mind of God. This is a gradual process and may take years (in earth consciousness of time) to fulfil. I feel as though I am starting on a Path of Light which leads upwards and onwards into Realms of unimaginable beauty and wonder and of which I have, as yet, but the faintest glimmer of comprehension. The journey itself is compensation enough for the trials of earth existence and for the emotion of judgment in action of those trials and of my individual response to them, from which judgment I am now emerging. I am reminded of a passage of Robert Browning:

"There shall never be one lost good! What was shall live as before. . . . On the earth the broken arcs, in the heaven, a perfect round. All we have willed or hoped or dreamed of good shall exist; not its semblance, but itself; no beauty, nor good, nor power whose voice has gone forth but each survives for the melodist when eternity affirms the conception of an hour. The high that proved too high, the heroic for earth too hard, the passion that left the ground to lose itself in the sky are music sent up to God by the lover and the bard. Enough that he heard it once; we shall hear it by and by."

PART II

Explanation

[Helen Greaves]
Between these two series of scripts was a period of nearly seventeen months. I had little or no communication with Frances during that time. Indeed I was quite certain in my mind that Frances had finished her inspiration for the book. I felt that she had truly 'gone on'; that she was out of reach of my mind, and because of this belief I never thought of contact with her.

Once, during a Meditation Session at a Conference of the Churches' Fellowship for Psychical & Spiritual Studies which I attended and which was being led by our Chairman, Colonel Lester, I had a distinct 'vision' of Frances. This was not the Frances I had known, nor was it the Spirit I had 'seen' clairvoyantly in her habit when she was present at her own Memorial Service in London. This was a different Being, a Spirit filled with Light, radiant and glorious. She stood near the altar of the chapel where we were gathered for this prayer and meditation and Light streamed about her. I distinctly recall that her robe impressed me. It was of a light soft blue and it sparkled and shone. I can only compare its irridescence to a gown covered with spangles which caught and reflected light. Her face was the face of a young woman. She looked breathtakingly beautiful.

"Frances has found her soul" I thought, or heard inwardly. "She is her real self now."

From this pinnacle of achievement I did not, therefore, expect to have any more communication. Thus I was astounded when, early in September 1967, I became aware again of Frances' vibrations. For a few days I had known in my Inner Self that a Presence was about me. This is always revealed to me by the hushed expectancy with which I break off my ordinary everyday chores. This consciousness can arise at any time of the day. It seems, then, that I am switched into another world, another dimension. Sometimes a Messenger comes with the answer to an unspoken query; sometimes I experience a sense of great peace and oneness. But at length I felt sure that this was Frances and that she wished to write again. One evening I took my pen and notebook, composed myself and sat quiescent awaiting the message.

Nothing happened! I decided that I must have been mistaken.

But again came the sense of urgency. This went on for a few days, finally I telephoned a member of our own special Meditation Group which Frances and I had founded eight years before and which we still carry on. I asked for help.

"Will you and the other members 'tune in' and ask that, if there is a communication to be made, that my 'channel' may be cleansed and cleared so that Frances can reach me?" I asked. They promised their prayers and their thoughts.

The following weekend, when I was eating my Sunday lunch and listening to the radio my thoughts and attentions entirely occupied with the news, I stood up, went over to my desk, picked up pen and notebook and switched off the radio.

"Frances." Her name rang in my mind. I sat down and began to write, with my half-eaten lunch on the table beside me.

I finished transcribing the words that had come into my mind and read them through. They came from Frances—without a doubt. This was the first of the scripts that follow. They came spasmodically. I could see that they were different in content from the former communications. Frances had indeed stepped forward and upward. Her thoughts were more confident. She had found her true place. She was a soul reborn. Confirmation that this was so was given me later in the same month.

On 20th September I was fortunate to have a private sitting with a well known and excellent sensitive, Mrs. Lilian Bailey. This sitting had been 'booked' anonymously for almost four months, but it is interesting that it materialised at this special time. After encouraging messages of a personal nature from my husband and other dear ones, and directions about the book already published, *The Dissolving Veil*, and others to be published, I asked if my 'Friend' was present. The answer came without pause.

"This is a lady and she has stepped back while others communicated" said Mrs. Bailey. "Wait a minute. She is a little giddy, as she is taking on the conditions with which she left this life. She had a malignancy which finally spread over her body and she passed in a coma."

We sat quiet for a moment, then the sensitive said:

"That is over now and she is well and happy." She gave the name Frances and added "Some called her 'Fanny'." This was true as the reader can see for himself in the short biography I have added to this work. Her students in Africa called her Fanny. She knew this and it amused her, so that I was not surprised when she added, via the sensitive, "I am still the same Fanny!" Mrs. Bailey described Frances as having very lovely eyes, large luminous and grey. Those who knew her will testify that her eyes were beautiful.

"She is speaking of a book. She is very much in this book. In fact *she* is writing it" Mrs. Bailey went on, and I thrilled at the confirmation. "You often think of her." Then she gave other facts by which Frances could prove her identity.

Presently Mrs. Bailey's Guide spoke solemnly:

"This lady *has found her soul*". I felt joyful. "You must not expect her around. She has gone on, but she will be 'sending through' to you from time to time. She now has a more rapid rate of vibration than before. Because your own rate of vibration is rapid it is easy for her to come to you from time to time, but not all the time. She has not gone out of your life. She has found the wondrous beauty of Life beyond her capability of telling you. She is trying to say: 'What man has created in the Spheres is beyond anything man has created on earth'. She is now in the Creative Sphere."

How true was this I was to realise in the scripts that came through again in the following October, the last on her birthday, 10th December. They radiate a spiritual attainment that is the Spirit of Hope itself to me, and I trust, to those who read them.

Here then are the 'last' scripts written from a Higher Sphere.

Second Series of Scripts

I recall once your solemn remark "I would rather talk than eat". That day we had been talking. One of our long sessions, do you remember, a mutual friend was debating about joining the Churches' Fellowship for Psychical & Spiritual Studies (by the way I now think that the second adjective should be 'mystical') and we felt that it was the absolutely right and only thing for her to do, to guide her future work. In your little study we talked, discussed, formulated pros and cons, even concentrated our thoughts to help her to see the right course. That was a day of talk and it ended, do you recall, in our hearing that the necessary step had been taken. An interesting and exciting day. I did not fully appreciate then the power and scope of mind communicating with mind, as now I do. Nor the Reality and Purpose of the Soul Mind infiltrating Its knowledge of the next step in the Divine Plan. Then I 'saw through a glass darkly' but now, at least more clearly without the veil of the personality shrouding the truth which the soul knows but which the earth-born entity refuses to accept.

You would rather talk than eat. That still amuses me. Perhaps that is why I want to let you know that here we talk and talk though we do not need to eat in the same sense in which we took food into our bodies in the earth life. Yet our 'talk' is different. Here our 'conversations' consist of a 'communing'. Mind speaks to mind. On earth we made sounds, formulated words with varying vibrations or with different meanings and we employed tonal emphasis to express our purpose. In this further Life speech as sound is not needed. Vibration is everything. It is sufficient that we formulate and 'breathe out' a strong thought for this to communicate itself to other minds. We give and receive thought impressions. They carry our true meaning so that deceptive words cannot imply other than what we think, as is the case with much of the word sound of the personality. What a pity, you will say, that this is not the common order in earth life, where idle talk can cause strife and bitterness.

When, therefore, in the course of my communications to you I make use of the words 'I said', 'He said' you will realise that I am merely reiterating a turn of phrase which was usual in my personality life and which you, and those who read this will appreciate, because you are accustomed to it. But in very truth I now live in a state of 'deep communications'. My mind is caught up into the tenor of greater Minds. I am enabled, though not fully as yet, to listen to the wisdom distilled from advanced sources by both individual question and answer by Group teaching.

For I have now passed on from my spate of service in the Home to becoming one of a Group—in other words: to take my place as a newcomer, a very humble, ignorant one, in what I like to call an Extension Group. This is a group working in what you would term 'mysticism' and what we here ennoble by the title of Reality. This is only a name to differentiate it from the numbers of other Groups which form themselves into working companies for varying motives, e.g. Groups for Science and Scientific Development; Groups for Medicine and Healing Techniques for the human body; Groups to study the projection of a method for a wider reach of the human mind; Groups for evolutionary world patterns, for the study of the Creative Plan, for the animal and mineral kingdoms and more advanced Groups for reconciliation of the known history of the human race (Akashic records) with present and future trends and for possible alignment of Plans to advance evolution of animal man to spiritual man. There are, of course, states of being and awareness and groups of advanced entities far beyond my comprehension, for 'In my Father's House are many Mansions'!

Suffice it for one who has struggled and failed often to behold the Light clearly on earth, to have found a niche where Those who have Beheld and are ever Beholding can impart the richness and depth of Their Wisdom to a searching soul.

"You would rather talk than eat!"

For me now in my new state, *talk is food*. Communion with the Group and with the great souls at its Centre is my nourishment, my bread and wine, my staff of true Life.

11th September

Expansion. That is the key word now in this phase of my existence as a soul. We still live in an expanding universe and I emphasise the word still because we always have inhabited this world and the death of the physical sheath only serves to clear our vision. The world of the physical is expanding, changing endlessly, though most souls in that state of physical existence cannot make the link with the ephemeral personality strong enough to be able to realise that expansion. Even when the personality which, contrary to some beliefs, does survive death in a more attenuated form, is released into conscious expansion, it still exists. In an entity which had become deeply sunk into the illusion of material existence, or which has never developed the mental body of thought, nor made any contact with the soul, this new state of existence can be one of extreme difficulty and confusion. This explains why there are differing states or Planes of expansion here, as I tried to show in my former communications from the Home. The Shadow Lands do exist for those who cannot accept release from the imprisoned self, and in these shadows, the poor entities remain until they themselves wish to find other and lighter abodes.

We always possess a soul-body, or, can I put it another way, a soul extends out to each of us, but for millions of those in physical incarnation the link with the soul body is so ephemeral as to be almost non-existent. Thus, on arrival here, after the physical change called death, such entities find themselves naked to their brethren. That does not mean without clothing in the physical sense, but minus the protective and creative vibrations of the soul. It is as though they lacked an outer skin, also they no longer feel in command of themselves or their situation. They are lost and confused, therefore a prey to unprogressed entities who lurk in the shadows. Sometimes they feel still bound to familiar scenes of their earth life. Sometimes they exist in a semiconscious dream, whilst Helpers and loved ones await their return to awareness. The duration and density of this state must necessarily depend on the reality of materialism to them, i.e. the glamour of earth life, the illusion of the temporal state. A good man or woman, kindly, unselfish, seeking God during life, yet without knowledge or understanding of survival, has nothing to fear. His good deeds have already attracted those who can guide and help him to adjust to these new conditions and, under instruction, he will learn the aspirational approach to the soul.

That brings me to what I am trying to convey of Expansion in this realm. The soul expands its knowledge and wisdom into the surviving personality. This process may be disseminated over long periods of earth time . . . sometimes even hundreds of your earth years, according to the progression, or non-progression of the entity. But always there are Brethren of the Way to assist one who desires progress. The desire originates in the entity itself after reparation has been made for wrongs done and existing lower passions have been cleansed, healed and released. When partial cleansing has been affected, the next step towards Light is Service and many dear souls spend their transition stages in service to those still living in the hells of their own creation. Such service, voluntary and compassionate, strengthens the link with the waiting Self. Yet always that Self waits to expand *into* the entity.

There are many facets to such expansion. Loving service is but one. The progressing entity is still in need of education into that knowledge and wisdom which the soul possesses and for this purpose, numbers of Groups exist here and, I am led to believe, function on every Plane. The progressing entity is drawn by the Law of Attraction to a Group progressed to that stage which will express, *for him*, the intensity of awareness which he is now capable of receiving.

All is expansion here, but expansion in stages. This Law is exact. No entity can propel itself forward into a Group until its emotional, mental and spiritual expansion at least is comparable with the *fringe* of that Group's awareness. This is an important statement. Think it well through to its conclusions. Here, illusion, glamour and self-deception are of no avail. One reveals what one is. One advertises oneself even in one's apparel. The mask has been shed with the physical body. The developing Light body, its dimness or its brilliance, is apparent, especially to members of the Group to which the quality of such Light permits graduation.

13th October

In my last communication to you I emphasised the thought 'One reveals what one is. One advertises oneself even in one's apparel'. Of course, if you examine an earth personality, the phrase holds good on that level also. Clothes revealeth man. Instinctively when in the body we formed judgments of people whom we met by their appearance at first, that is, the brightness or dullness of their dress, the choice of colour, style, their smartness or lack of neatness.

As above so below—the rules hold. Only on this level of consciousness dress and style are not created by those who lead fashions. We create that which clothes, i.e. surrounds us, from the residue of our thoughts, words, acts and aspirations which we have brought over with us. One begins to learn, and to apply, this Law of Creation from the moment of awareness of one's survival in another dimension. Sometimes there is considerable space from the moment of withdrawal from the physical body to the moment of awareness, such a space depending for its duration, as we have already mentioned, on the familiarity or non-familiarity of the entity with life after human transition, with belief or non-belief in persisting consciousness, the strength and tenacity of materialistic concepts and, of course, the records of the life just ended. But when such awareness becomes, so to speak 'settled' then dawns the realisation that one clothes oneself. During the first stages of this new and rather exciting consciousness, the pleasure of creating costumes and colours fulfills a need and is often much enjoyed. On the other hand, a dress which had acquired meaning on earth will be assumed, sometimes for the satisfaction of the soul, sometimes as a penance, and sometimes for the joy or peace the wearing of it had afforded the soul. During my service in the Home I dressed myself in the habit of the Order to which I had belonged on earth and in which, most of my fellow servers had also been professed. This was necessary to me for various private reasons though during some phases of this experience, I allowed myself the pleasure of creating the well-remembered colours and fashions of my later earth years.

At last came the opportunity to pursue the progress onwards which I so eagerly desired. By similarities of mind and aspiration I was 'drawn' towards a Group. Eagerly I 'communed' with them. My joy was deep and strong when I realised that I had, indeed, found my own Group even though I knew myself to be only on the outer fringe of their activities. And here may I emphasise the value of the Group consciousness which we had practised and struggled to attain together. The 'groove' which we had forged into our consciousness of Group responsibility at soul level, of unity at the Centre, of Group growth of the divine qualities into our composite whole, all this was of inestimable help in my entry into, and understanding of, the Law of Group work.

Gradually I became aware of my fellows as 'arrayed' in colours as in garments and by the depth or brightness or soberness or brilliance of their 'surround' I came to know, not only their characters, but their individual advance into the Spiritual Realms. This was indeed most revealing, yet humbling. I saw that now I must discard the habit to which I had clung. It had served its usefulness. *I must wear what I am as a garment.* The thought was terrifying. What was I? Dare I stand before my Group companions in the 'new habit' of my thought? Would the colours be sombre or bright? Long and earnestly I talked with others who were in very much the same predicament, and I meditated earnestly on what I wanted to be that such may be presented in truthful Light about me.

This is a new stage. I am still a neophite. It is the preparatory stage (concentration before meditation in the earthly technique) of working down into oneself to discover what one really is; the utterly honest summing up of one's faculties both mental and aspirational and then 'letting forth' of whatever Light has dawned, into a shape. 'Let your Light so Shine' has a solid meaning here.

Gradually the garment evolves, the colour settles, and you are arrayed as you really are. You have assumed your Light. In other words, the surviving personality is reunited with at least a part of the true Soul body.

Life excites you. Mind grows into clarity, expansiveness,

creativeness. YOU ARE. YOU LIVE. You can now take your rightful place in the Group, albeit only on the outer ring. Your
ascent into consciousness has begun. You are clothed in raiment
of Light as your fellows. Now your Light can mingle with their
brilliance and become One in intensity. Thought and aspiration grow into joy and ecstasy. Channels of wisdom and knowledge open to you, beauty becomes a living reality.

This is the 'breakthrough' I had longed for when in the
physical body. It never manifested in intensity then. Flashes of
awareness but served to deepen the hunger of the personality
for the soul's radiance. Perhaps this clarity of consciousness is
not possible in the materialism of earth life. I cannot know
the answer to that. All I realise now emphasises the reality
and practicality of Jesus' teaching. Within is the Kingdom of
Heaven. "Seek ye first the Kingdom of Heaven and all these
things shall be added unto you". All, all was within me then,
as now, but the veil of glamour and illusion barred my sight, as
it still veils Reality for most dwellers on the earth.

Dear Friend, this is but the initial stage of a Journey into
Light, during which the surviving entity is gradually reunited
with the whole soul. Step upon step into greater Light lies
ahead of me, yet truly it suffices. "One step enough for me. . . ."

14th October

In your mind I recognise questions about the Group. How
did I know that I belonged to this particular Group? How did
I contact the Group? What credentials had I which enabled me
to be accepted by the other members?

I realise that I too would have wanted to know the answers
had I received such communications from another mind working in a different state of consciousness. I will endeavour to
answer as clearly as I can. I will take your second query first.
How did I contact this Group?

This was not a case of contacting, as though, for the first
instance, this Group. From time immemorial it seems that I
have been attached to it. Now this is a reunion. Is this such a
mystery? Every soul has its place in the Divine Scheme of Living. Every soul belongs to a group and forms an integral part
of a Group soul. I do. You do. The meanest beggar in the street

does, the greatest genius does. A Group Soul is constituted of souls at individual levels of progress, each complementing the others to make a Whole. One is part of a Group Soul as one is part of a family in the physical sense; a family relationship may be temporary, but a soul relationship is eternal.

The question of twin souls, about which much nonsense and speculation is made on earth, can be explained by the hypothesis of two souls belonging to the same Group but drawn close in harmony because they are at equal stages of progression and because they have advanced conspicuously together. This gives them similar vibrations and a corresponding 'pull' of attraction. But all souls constituting a Group Soul experience this 'drawing together in harmony' towards each other, whether they are functioning in material bodies or are traversing the stages here in the Life of the Spirit. Group Souls preside over universal movements, over great causes and thus members of one Spiritual Family are often attracted to each other by mutual interests, by a special life work, as well as by eternal links. They work together, may indeed share their lives in partnership, or may only meet occasionally as they work in some particular project. Sometimes, by what appears to be a perverse fate, members of the same Group are separated, born into the apparently wrong camps. Their lives become tragic, often futile in their repeated efforts to rejoin their similar companions and their rightful work. Strangely enough many never find their right niche. Often they live and die as outcasts. But, as the entire complement of a Group Soul is never in complete incarnation at the same time, i.e. there is always an integrated part of the Group on this Side, the outcasts, after their transition here and after they have gained consciousness of their state and have attained to at least some measure of Light, rejoin their own Groups.

Now I am conscious of your mind enquiring "How many Group Souls are there?"

I cannot answer that. So far as I have gleaned their number must be uncountable. I also understand that, at higher levels of consciousness, Group Souls unite to form greater Units. This, I reason, must be the continued Law of Progress into Divinity which is a Unity, a Oneness, a total mysterious and glorious whole. But only thus far dare I aspire to the Divine Plan. Here and now I am privileged to be enabled to touch, only the fringe, of the consciousness of Groups working at this level and to co-operate with them.

To the extent therefore of my present comprehension I have endeavoured to reply to your question. You will appreciate, I trust, that no credentials as such (except my own aspiration and reparation for past wasted opportunities) were needed for entry into my Group. I was, so to speak, assimilated into it, for it was my rightful place.

How, you ask, was I brought into communion with this Group?

Do you recall that in the early communications from the Rest Home to which I first graduated for service, I recounted the story of a certain doctor, the surgeon who had, whilst in the earth body, fallen a victim to drug addiction? You remember that, with him, I visited a Group and was in communication with a number of advanced Souls. On several visits I met and communed with these Minds which have reached high standards of consciousness and wisdom. Sometimes they patiently explained Group workings to me. One, a fine and illumined Soul, instructed me . . . "Seek for your own place. Ask that Light may open your mind to that which is for you; that your vibratory rate may be increased to respond to the vibration of your Group; that you may become aware of them, for they are close beside you. . . ."

For long I meditated on these words.

Suddenly, as I looked upon my old friend Father Joseph when we were attending a patient in the Home, I beheld, not the usual brown habit with which I have always associated him, but a 'surround' of glorious blue which clothed him. It seemed that I looked right into him. My inner eyes were opened. I knew. His smile was gentle but all understanding as he said:

"My child, welcome home!"

The words were sufficient, the contact was made. It had been necessary for me to await enlightenment, but he had always known. I found it difficult to leave the Home and Mother Florence where I had been so happy. But the prospect of progress was inspiring. Besides, I was comforted by learning that Mother Florence would be visiting the Group to which I was going from time to time, as she too was one with it, yet perforce chose to remain at her duties in the Home until all her 'flock' had been safely welcomed to this side of Life.

I cannot make explicit to you the 'mechanics' of my move to the Group, partly because I yet am not entirely cognisant of all that occurred myself, and partly because there is no pocket of thought in your mind which could 'receive' such information. This I can offer for your comprehension and that of the readers; whilst I was meditating in my golden garden, I found myself 'transported' back to that Temple of Learning where once before, I dared to penetrate. Only this time, Father Joseph (I now know him by another name) was with me. Together we joined a cluster of entities about a Teacher. Immediately I experienced a rise of consciousness, an upsurge of joy, a mingling of unity and harmony which coloured my whole being. I cannot explain this in any other terms, though I doubt whether they will have the same connotation for you.

I knew this was right for me. I had come into my own. There was no definite acceptance, the entire operation was unobtrusive and simple, yet I had the conviction that all was well, that I was amidst my fellow-travellers on the Way.

"What is this Group called?" I flashed silently to Father Joseph. He smiled.

"What you have always sought, my child—Reality!"

Then I knew it for the extension of that reaching out for Spiritual Truth and Creative Force which, when on earth, we had termed 'mysticism'. Here was the first phase of the search for Mystical Union but on a higher level, and without the incubus of earth personality and the fluctuating interference of the fleshly desire body.

Have I answered your question?

15th October

This is the most satisfying stage of my progress through life and, I believe, lives, and the consequent reviewing of such lives, which my memory can, at present recall. I was always worrying, puzzling, searching in my earth life, as Frances Banks, as Sister Frances Mary and as Frances Banks again. I was never sure that I had truly found that for which I searched so eagerly. For twenty-five years in religion I tried earnestly to accept the concept of Truth to which I had vowed myself, but nobody can know the dark nights of the soul, the loneliness, the feeling of defeat through which frustration led me during those years. Sincerely and honestly though I endeavoured to believe in the life of the religious, my inner Voice always urged expansion of knowledge and experience. I loved my work of teaching. I believe my teaching qualities could be assessed as good. I liked knowledge for its own sake and led a useful life no doubt, in the place to which I had been assigned. But ever the Spirit goaded me 'Seek and ye shall find'.

When, however, the way opened for me and I was allowed to leave the Order after my vows were annulled, I discovered, as we all have to discover, that the open, sunny paths down which we seem pressed to venture have bogs of despair and morasses of doubt, as well as vistas of promise. At least, I felt then, that I was moving, not stagnating, as life seemed to have become in the Order.

But moving where? Often I wearied myself with conjecture. I pleaded and prayed for Light yet the full consummation of its glory always eluded me. In my latter years I found a silent awareness in meditation; a new resolving of self with Self and a resulting confidence to speak out concerning this search to others. In the few Retreats for the Churches' Fellowship which I led, the exercise and discipline of preparation, and many hours were spent in this, were real spiritual gain for me. If I was blessed enough to have been able to impart, even a few flashes of insight that I had gained in these mental and spiritual gropings, then a star of hope was kindled on my own way.

Now that I have left behind the dark veils which blind the spiritual insight during one's earthly pilgrimage, I find that I am still repeating the pattern, only from another angle. No longer do I doubt as once I did. Now I know. Yet, with all honesty I have to admit that Reality appears, at times, too wonderful even for my growing and expanding consciousness. Do I dream—I ask myself, and shall I, one morning, awake?

It might surprise you to learn that this reaction is a common one amongst the pilgrims I have met. The mind, you see, is only slowly, very slowly, opening to its vast potential. The veils of matter which now, to us, are represented by a loss in frequency of vibration have, so recently, been dissolved that we can and do proceed only into each successive stage with deepening understanding and a widening of conscious awareness. To put this idea into the language and metaphor of the earth world, it is as if each Cinderella had, inexplicably, become a Princess.

You will want to know more of my occupations, living arrangements and I will do my best to explain simply, so that you and those who read, may comprehend, at least in part, some of the spiritual satisfactions which are so much integrated into one's journey onwards.

I have a new home. I share a beautiful estate with others of the Group. This place has wide sloping grass lands, trees and flowers of the most exquisite beauty and avenues of Light, I have no other words for this, for meditation and contemplation. As we here are closer in vibration to the Spiritual Worlds, the echoes of the music of the spheres along these avenues becomes a glory sweeping our thoughts and aspirations into contemplation of the Mystery of Divinity and Eternal Life.

We are free, of course, to follow our own pursuits. There are no college rules or compulsory attendances but I, for one, find myself at the Halls of Learning almost continually. Again, you notice, I repeat the pattern, that avid desire for spiritual knowledge, which I now realise characterised all my excursions into different experiences on earth, and which I now comprehend, albeit vaguely as having been the focus of those personalities with which I have returned to incarnation. This avidity may not be an asset!

I can travel in the mind and this I often do. I have visited countries of the world which I did not know. I have seen much and learned much. I return often to familiar scenes. I attend some Meetings and Meditation Groups and sometimes contact the friends and companions I had loved on earth. I do not find it an easy matter to 'speak through' a medium. As you appreciate, I have the conviction that there is no necessity for this. On this level of thought, telepathy is developed to a greater potential than was practised on earth. By means of thought transference, I endeavour to reach the minds of old and dear friends still in physical existence. Sometimes I am happy to think that my efforts meet with a certain response. At others the veil of illusion (even in those who should know better) interferes with reception and the contact is faulty, or is even rejected. But this will be so whilst those on earth still cling to the theory of separativeness.

That which I am learning here, in this wider state of consciousness, is a joyous apprehension of the vast wonder of the unity of Creative Mind in which all, every atom, every soul-fragment, every Group Soul, every creative thought, is One.

10th December

This will be my last script for the book. If there is a message in these writings it is the simple statement that all is Unity and that Unity is Light.

That statement may be interpreted symbolically by my readers as referring to the Light of Wisdom, of Knowledge, of Understanding of the Unity of the Life in all things. But a difficult point I would try to make clear is that, in this further phase of our existence on this plane, the reference to Light is to be interpreted *literally*. We are progressing into Light and yet more Light. To us now, references to the 'Golden Throne of God' which formed part of our religious instruction on earth, now reveal definite hidden Truths. The Utmost of such Light is beyond our comprehension, which is still limited, or even our highest aspirations.

Light here is literally the substance and matter of our thought life. Thus, as our thoughts become attuned to the vibration of Creative Divinity, so the substance of our bodies changes, becoming less dense and reflecting more Light.

We carry our own Light. The greater therefore the selflessness and illumination of our minds and the more positive our response to the higher frequency of vibration, the purer and brighter is the Light transmitted by us.

We spoke of the Group Soul.

Thus, as I begin to comprehend now, the purer and stronger the Light from each unit soul of the Group, the greater the advancement of the Group Soul Itself towards ultimate bliss of Union, towards that ineffable Light which will ever be the mystery and wonder of Divinity.

Yet each 'unit' must be proved, i.e. its Light must be subjected to the test of veils of density in other spheres of action.

So many units return again and again to the nothingness of dense matter, bravely asserting the lasting reality of their illumination. So often such units, clothed in their passing personalities, fall into ignorance, becoming subject to materialistic concepts. Some are blessed on their journeys by flashes into the Light, and in rare cases, the Light gained in these spiritual Worlds holds steady, shining through the fleshly masks to bless and encourage their fellow travellers in the darkness of supposed separativeness. Light shines from the eyes of these advanced egos, and is reflected in the magnetic fields which surround their dense bodies.

Perhaps my greatest regret now is the realisation that, whilst I was seeking and searching mentally, psychically and occultly to discover that 'breakthrough' to spirit for which I longed, the Light of the Unity with all things, all creatures, all Beings, all Hosts, all Powers dwelt within me in ineffable glory.

'I am the Light of the World' means just that.

Jesus, the Master, reflected that Light pure and untrammelled during His dwelling in the density of crude matter. The Light dwells in all of us as a shining effulgence, the Light of Oneness with all Spirit, the blessed awareness and acknowledgement of unity with all creation from the lesser to the Higher Orders, even to the Throne of Grace Itself.

'Let your Light so shine before men . . .' is essentially a fact here where each is revealed by his light.

May it be true then, of those who read these words on earth. May the Light of Awareness of Divine Unity shine through the illusive and temporal veils of assumed personalities, so that, in preparation for this further experience, they may indeed be known by their Light.

God Bless You all.

December 1967 (Sussex)